MW00441137

The Circus Train

Also by Judith Kitchen

Essays
Half in Shade: Family, Photography, Fate
Distance and Direction
Only the Dance: Essays on Time and Memory

Novel
The House on Eccles Road

Poetry
Perennials

Critical Study
Writing the World: Understanding William Stafford

Editor
Short Takes: Brief Encounters with Contemporary
    Nonfiction

Co-Editor
The Poets Guide to the Birds, with Ted Kooser
In Short: A Collection of Brief Creative Nonfiction,
    with Mary Paumier Jones
In Brief: Short Takes on the Personal, with Mary
    Paumier Jones

THE CIRCUS TRAIN

Judith Kitchen

OVENBIRD

Ovenbird Books, 2013

Port Townsend, WA

Copyright © 2013 by Judith Kitchen.
All rights reserved.

If you would like to use material from this book (other than for review purposes), prior permission must be obtained by contacting the author through ovenbirdbooks.org. Thank you for your support of the author's rights.

Cover art: "Night Train" by William Kitchen

OVENBIRD

Ovenbird Nonfiction Series

Ovenbird Books
ovenbirdbooks.org

Library of Congress Cataloging-in-Publication Data is on file.
ISBN: 1940906008
ISBN 13: 9781940906003

for Stan,
for my family and friends,
for all my company

The Circus Train

How through memory a person is one,
and how without it there is no more I,
or at least a continuous I . . .

—Joseph Joubert, 1800

Start at the toes. Eternally cold.

Ever since the chemo leaked, your toes have had no feeling. So start there. This is the beginning. Eternal. Cold. A dizzying loss of balance.

In Samuel Beckett's *Company*, memory persists. A long walk up a hill, holding his mother's hand. Until she drops it. But still, he returns to that moment, again and again. The walk. The hand.

There's something I have to say about the good properties of metastasis. It's certain. There's no backing out, so you are forced to accept. It's a little bit like that column of dust in the old Westerns, far in the distance, but announcing its presence as it takes its interminable time coming closer and closer until, suddenly, there it is with a shape and the horse gallops up hard in your face and stops still, all lathery, and you know you are just about to hear some news of some sort. From then on, it's all first person. Or sort of.

Mid-May. The apple trees in the yard behind our house have blossomed so that, waking, I look into a sea of white clouds. I could go back to apple trees, the peculiar branchings that make for good climbing, my mother's voice calling me down. Instead, I see a young girl alone, crouched on a hot day in early June, sifting the dirt of the strawberry patch. Each runner shoots out its individual white flower. Tiny, tinged with pink. But I am intent on the sifting, the sun a poultice on my neck, warm and filled with silence. Each ray streaks upward toward its source. In front of me, a soft pile of sifted dirt, silken, the texture of talc. My hand smoothes and smoothes it, leaving little trails of fingermarks. My hair pulls loose from my braids and makes a haze of sunlight around my head. The breeze is softer than the dirt, like a finger brushed over the forehead. I do not remember what I was thinking, but *that* I was thinking. Alone with my thoughts. With the dirt and the breeze and my own sense of self that did not disappear with my mother's call.

I am sitting up in bed and the dark is palpable around me. It breathes in and out, a faint echo of my own heavier breathing. Not quite a wheeze—more like a sigh, each breath holding an almost audible sound. I am awake from a dream in which I have informed my mother—who was, as usual, being secretive—that I was going to leave if she wouldn't admit that I was going to die. This feels like an important dream, and one that I will probably have again. So I am sitting here in the dark, reliving its details, reliving, in short, my life.

The walk. The hand. One detail, over and over. As though his life could be summed up.

I remember too much. Not everything, but enough that it feels like dredging up the past in all its textures and colors and odors and sounds. What was said, when, why. The table, with its jumble of plates and silverware, his hand reaching but still, my eyes full of tears. They wash over me now, thirty years later, more, and still the words remain unsaid, and still I hear the chatter of the other people around us, the seemingly incredible lightness of its being. And still, even after all these years, I wish it different, wish to hear it unfold in some other fashion, wish for my life to have branched out from that moment—which of course it did, just a slightly different branch of a slightly different life lived in a slightly different way because of what did not transpire.

The sun is a shawl. A smattering on the arms, making them smart with the wildness of July. But this is June. The dirt is the soft shade of shale, of fallow fields after wheat has given over to stubble. The strawberries themselves are still to come, but the blossoms persist, white stars along the runners that weave over the interstices between the rows. Cut through—shortcuts, like dendrites—to other worlds. This is the place where memory begins.

THE CIRCUS TRAIN

Or does it? Because I have earlier memories—vivid, narrative, filled with action. I remember the pink and white dress, the black Oldsmobile with its running-board, the men from the CO camp, the snake they killed and threw onto the fence where it withered in the sun, the cows lowing in the Erwins' barn, the clank of their stanchions, the mossy underside of the woods where sometimes we found a jack-in-the-pulpit hiding discreetly among the leaves, my father's trusty three-speed bicycle, the stab of pain in my broken collar bone, the careful inching out as you walked up the seesaw and then the sudden whoosh as it tipped, hurtling you down again to another beginning. All of these are before, but all of these happened *to* me. In the strawberry patch, I was the one making things happen. Especially in my head, my thinking, my careful tune of a thought.

I wonder, will that be the last thing to go? For so many people, thought goes first, and they live out the remainder in a haze of happening. What day is this? Or, who called? Did you say you called? What is for dinner? Do I like that? A confusion of time and place and incident. But I will

be young—younger—and my mind intact.
So will thought be my solace, or my curse?
I have relied on the brain—its tickings and
tockings—for an entire lifetime. Can I trust
it to take me easily into death, or will it
resist, fighting the body until the bitter end?

I looked up, and there
it was—the little circus train winding
through the valley. But was there a valley? I
don't remember that there was. There were
cornfields, and beyond them the woods.
And the river on the other side of the road.
But I remember the train, far away, while I
was sitting in the strawberry patch. It must
have been another time, another place. But
there it is: the blue and yellow and laven-
der cars following the tiny plume of smoke,
rounding a bend, suddenly emerging from
a string of trees, making its bright way
across the horizon—well, not horizon, but
the landscape below it, pulling the animals
and acrobats and jugglers from somewhere
to somewhere else. I see it so clearly, almost
seventy years later, and still there is doubt
because I see the house, the apricot tree, the
strawberry patch, and there is no room in
that scene for the little valley with its tiny
chugging circus. I knew what was in those

cars—the clowns with their floppy shoes and the wrinkly elephants and the magical tent. The tightrope walker, his suddenly humdrum gravity. Knew it so well I could worm my way inside to discover the smell of straw and the sound of fatigue. Knew, even then, that it was hard work, bringing their magic to children like me. Work, and disappointment, and the heart lifting a bit as the little train passed over a bridge, leaving the valley behind. So where . . .

Memory serves her well. And yet here, caught on the brink of its own oblivion, it deserts her at a crucial moment. That train has lived in the folds of her brain for well over half a century, and only now, when she wanted to write it down, did it disappear into ripples of doubt. She sees it now, the noisy engine silently pulling through the distance of her dream, and the colorful cars painted in reds and greens and pastels, a moving rainbow that seems, in memory, to blend with the silken dirt and the smell of impending summer and her fifth birthday looming. This was before the flood, and the valley was opulent, new corn coming up, and the river a strip of sunlight flashing on, then off, as she moved her head.

JUDITH KITCHEN

It was Beckett who said, "Fail again. Fail better." That's about as optimistic as he gets, and if you think about it, that's fairly optimistic. It carries something more than his usual view of human nature. If you can have a "better," then failure isn't as failed as all that.

He held my hand across the table, but his eyes looked away. He held my hand, but it was as solace, not as entreaty. Oh, I remember other times, his hand reaching for mine, tipping the wine into my lap. Laughter. But those were later. And they could not—quite—erase the moment his hand held nothing for me. The way his touch was more than I could bear in its absence.

Was the train in a book— a picture book, so that its colors persist as though they were trailing each other across the page? It could be. Books were that real. But I was sitting in the strawberry patch, with only my eyes to take in my red-and-white-striped overalls, my bare feet, the white confetti of the blossoms. Picture perfect. Except for the valley that didn't exist. But it *did* exist, because we lived there. Nowhere to look but out. And up.

THE CIRCUS TRAIN

So where . . .

My Aunt Margaret clacks her castanets and sings, her skirts moving like water, her dark hair piled on her head and held with the stem of a flower. A red flower. An orange skirt. A blouse embroidered with blue and yellow stitching. She has just returned from a year with the American Friends Service Committee in Ecuador and Guatemala. She is singing in another language and the notes wrap me in their gaudy sounds and the castanets chatter. Aunt Margaret is back, and even the house seems to quicken its ears with her laughter. She stamps her feet, *Ta-dah*, with an emphasis on the *dah* that leaves an impressive silence in its wake.

White house in the valley, on River Road. White house with a garden. And the woods beyond. Woods where I learned the oily scent of wintergreen. Its stringent aftertaste. Its red berries in winter. Patch of woods bright in my mind, my father pointing, saying over and over the names for what we were seeing. White house. River Road. Chemung River. Erwin's

JUDITH KITCHEN

Dairy. Holstein and Guernsey. Strawberry. Apricot. Lady's-slipper, pink inside pink.

And then we moved. The names changed. Hamilton Street. How did a street differ from a road? Well, the road moved on, wound through the contours of landscape. The street plowed through, straight as a needle, marching itself into town. Oh, behind us it went up the hill, but it went straight, as though the hill were merely impediment. And the town rose up, two blocks away, not taller exactly, but with steeples and drugstores and wide cement buildings full of groceries and, even wider, the two-block stretch of factory with its deep noon whistle, its men spilling out into the park with their domed metal lunch pails and thermoses full of hot, black coffee. And then they packed up the waxed paper that had wrapped their sandwiches and the cores of their apples and screwed on the lids of their thermoses and clicked closed the lids of their lunch boxes and hauled themselves out of the green park benches and walked back through the door where darkness swallowed them whole. And you skated past them on roller skates, or rode past on your fat-wheeled bike, and you knew nothing of their lives but that noontime exodus, and that resigned sigh as they stood up to resume the rest of their day. And you turned right on Water Street and wheeled past the courthouse on to where the concrete dike held the river at bay. You dropped your bike to the grass and straddled the wall and then walked its six-inch width—twenty, thirty, forty feet, before you dropped to the other side where the marsh smelled of cattails gone to seed, and your voices carried and you were caught up in the freedom of being where you were not allowed to go.

The body high in the maple tree. Looking out, through new eyes. The neighborhood small, smaller than you had expected it to be. The sidewalks all lined up to take you places, but here you are, gone up instead of out. Up to where the leaves are your intimates. Up past the natural crook where your body can fit safely into this higher perch where everything is precarious. Above the roof. Above the neighboring tree. Where wind can find you.

Such a short time. From the top of that tree to this white chair before the white desk. A blink. A cough. Wind finds you out.

JUDITH KITCHEN

Windswept, windblown, downwind, wind down. Wind at my back, sword in my side, sidewinder, winding sheet, wraparound gown, wound up, simple past tense of the wound that I carry, surgical scar that confounds me day after day after uncertain day.

I see the four-year-old Beckett. An Irish town, rowhouses tightly knit on each side, and the little shops distinguishing themselves with signs for butcher, bakery, newsagent, post office. His mother grasps his hand to keep him from straying. But now they are on their way home and the shops are thinning and women are out cleaning their stoops and his mother drops his hand to shift her purchases so they settle a bit more comfortably in her white string bag and he skips on ahead, pulled up the hill by some invisible magnetism and then, when he's gone a bit too far, he realizes he is no longer holding her hand and, even though he waits for her to catch up, she does not reach for him, and he will remember that fact for the rest of his life.

Just as you will remember the swirl of the water as it rounded the curve of the river and the *chit chit terr-eeee* of redwing blackbirds and the wash of minnows over your toes. Just as you will remember the back yard a carpet of reds and yellows, and your mother looking out, unable to see you up there in the October leaves. Just as you will continue to hear her calling, and your answering silence, smug in those leaves, alone with your sense of the power of your silence.

Of course you could go on replaying scene after scene. But to what end? Don't these moments disappear with you, drop off into the void? You suspect that they do—and so you write them furiously, as though you could hang on to a lifetime when, in fact, you know you can't. Can't ever quite add it up and make it make sense and make its sum be something—some *thing*—you can hand over, relieve yourself of, bequeath.

Here is a mystery: what do the spent days do with themselves? How do they breathe in the face of forgetfulness? They have names, and faces. They can't just be erased. Do you hear that? You should try to hold on. I want you to hold on, if only for my sake. So my days, too, will inflate your lungs. Will fill them with this crisp autumn air that I can breathe at will, at the will of my recollection.

We've just finished watching the 2012 World Cup qualifier between Chile and Argentina, and I realize I've been blessed to watch Lionel Messi, easily the world's best player. The ball moved so fluidly, like a needle through cloth. And Messi poured through the defense, even more fluid—a stream of proficiency. That's not to say in 2014 I'll root for Argentina. No, I'll be solidly for Brazil because I was also blessed to watch Pelé, whose career was just winding down when I moved there. I didn't exactly like Brazil, but it's impossible to hate a place that can produce a Pelé. Where *having fun* is more important than *getting done.* Where the sound of the samba moves like a snake up the hillside and the sun finds you out wherever you are.

So many things to remember, so why do I think of Matthew, who was just over four, trailing through the rooms with an old towel safety-pinned around his neck, a haphazard paper crown, and stocking feet? After a while, he would lie down on the sofa, fold his hands carefully over his heart, and close his eyes. "What are you doing?" we asked. "I'm being Dom Pedro." What did we expect? He'd been there in Petrópolis when we'd taken off our shoes and slid our feet into pale blue paper slippers—like the ones surgeons wear—to make our way slowly in line past the carved pews and gold platters and the sculpted images of Brazil's founding fathers, past Dom Pedro's sarcophagus, the great ruler laid out in all his granite finery, finally at home. Never mind that, while we lived there, the country was ruled by a dictator. People still went to the beach and drank infinite cups of *cafezinho*. Though it's hard to explain what it was like to live inside a language you didn't fully own. Or to discover that incessant sun is like incessant rain. Or to go in fear of mistakes after one of your friends found his car riddled with bullets when he got lost one night driving home. Or, ultimately, to be afraid of the beach itself—its broiling sun and its drowning waves, the fact that people came armed with candles in case someone died. Or, simply, to wonder why you never could learn the words to the songs.

JUDITH KITCHEN

Distance does give perspective—in time as well as space. For example, in Bahia, that wheelbarrow full of blood and intestines was, at the time I encountered it, almost more than I could take. I mean, they sloshed. Blood dripped down the sides. It was coming right at me. But now, over thirty years later—no, over forty—that wheelbarrow has become quite tame. The colors have faded. It moves in slow motion. I'm not saying that it isn't as real, but that it's more real, dredged up as part of what adds up to the images of my life. There I am, just over thirty, my long brown hair pulled back, the bright sky hovering over all those whitewashed churches, the market a boil of sound, and then there it is—seething red reality, but somehow stilled—something that will return and return to be sure I understand that life has its inner worlds as well.

She sees her reflection in the store window. She looks at herself and I stare back. Or I look at myself and she stares back. It's hard to tell which. I am older and she is young. Or vice versa. She seems to have startled herself. Who are we, now that we have to rely on new ways of calculating the integers of time?

THE CIRCUS TRAIN

Her son William has written a song. He says it is about love. He says her love has sustained him. There are tears in his voice. She remembers him, a young father, taking care of his son. More alone than she has ever been. His love sustained his son. If that is a part of her, she will own it. She will remember him walking the streets with an infant in a carriage. No song but the rain.

To own experience feels important these days. To record it. Not for posterity, but for the present self who pretends to notice things intently the way someone facing death is supposed to, but who really just chugs along in her daily grind and wishes she were even more involved in the process of living. So now, here I am, writing it down—how when we arrived Simon was busily tying his tie. He's nine, for god's sake, and he was wearing a striped shirt and a red tie. His long red hair kept falling over his eyes and he had to flick it back, but boy, was he dressed to the nines, no pun intended. At dinner—at Mrs. Turner's Hometown Café—Simon whispered, "I thought we might go somewhere fancy. I was so freaked out, because my dress pants were dirty."

JUDITH KITCHEN

Dress pants? He's nine, for god's sake. Fancy? Well, that I can understand. He doesn't get to do fancy very often, and he's trying on another life. I'd try on another life if I could. Step right out of this body and into another. I'd like to see what things look like through other eyes, whether what holds my attention now would hold my attention then. But how would I know? I mean, I'd be someone else, with just a hint of something following me, ghostlike, as though something felt familiar . . . but why, and how?

As she lay dying—she loves when she can make a literary allusion—she thought about what her life had meant, and in the end it didn't add up. There was more positive than negative, more success than failure, more love than hate, but still, it didn't add up. Not the way it does in a good novel. With insight. Or closure. And that's the way of it—the way life goes on and on, infinitely unending. It ends, but not with ending. And then the potent antibiotics began to work, and slowly—more slowly than those omnipresent clocks ticking down ten minutes in movie time that take half an hour in what we'd call real time, more slowly than waiting for someone you know will not call to call, more slowly than sewing a quilt, or walking on sand, or hoping against hope—she began to improve.

You are young, under seven, and you and George are staying with the Days while your parents are out of town. The Days have four children, and so it's usually fairly easy to get lost in the crowd. For the most part, you have a good time. But not when Nancy Day—the mother—decides it's time for the daily interrogation as to who has, or has not, had a bowel movement. You don't know how to force a bowel movement, so she always threatens you with castor oil. Her daughter—the only girl—is older than you. She's also named Nancy, which seems strange to you, and they've resorted to calling her Cookie, so they gave her a name they can't even use. Cookie has long brown hair that she wears in braids and you inherit most of her clothes—except the ones that Nancy saves in case she should ever have another girl. When her next baby is Freddie, she lets his blond hair grow long and puts him in a pink dress for a photograph before she has it cut. Anyway, Cookie tells you that all you have to do is say you did whether you did or not. This seems so simple you can't imagine why you never thought of it. You've been freed of a worry that circled your head all day. Emancipated. Cookie's hand-me-down dress becomes your favorite. You want some of its wisdom to wear off.

I've been toying with the idea of going through the photo albums looking for an angle at which I might have seen that circus train. Maybe I'll realize that it was there—in that valley—after all, but that I wasn't in the strawberry patch when I saw it. I've conflated two memories, but they remain memories. That's what I'm hoping. Otherwise, I will become someone who makes up a memory—and I am uncomfortable with that. I've relied on my memory all of my life—to confirm, yes, but also to limit and locate and, well, relive. To give me back to myself. There I am, around five years old, following that thin line of smoke. Pushing my way into those pastel cars with their silver costumes—a bit grimier than they appear from the distance of the audience— and their shiny boots. Pushing my way to where the cages of animals hold an incipient roar. Here I am, remembering my way back into imagination, as that girl stands so still, letting the train slip out of sight. She is my ticket to time long gone, and I need her to look so hard and stand so still that I can feel her inside me. That I can know—for sure—what all of this living has been about.

Actually, Beckett had asked his mother whether the sky was more distant than it appeared, and in response she had shaken off his hand. Not dropped it to rearrange the groceries, but shaken it off, to indicate disapproval. And Beckett, the old man, lies on his back in the dark and calls up the time his mother shook off his hand. Calls up a life where that one act—rejection—has persisted across time, and space, even language. Has formed itself like a pebble in the shoe, or a mole on the back, something that cannot be seen, but still it agitates.

Here's what I want: to stitch it all together. Give it the dilated eye of attention. To make it add up. But of course it doesn't add up, no more than any other life. We take from the box of photos those that lead, one to another. We leave behind the singular, solitary moments that go nowhere except into, and out of, themselves. I remember once

when Frank Day—the father—took us all for
a ride in his convertible. The needle began to
climb its arc across the dashboard—40, 50,
60, 70, 80 mph. In 1950, that was too fast.
Each curve would throw us together, sliding across the bench seat in unison, feeling
a bit the way you felt when the lead skater
stopped and the rest of you, holding hands,
were tugged on around him, thrown out into
the slippery cold. I was afraid and I told my
mother about 80 mph. We did not stay with
the Days after that. I don't know what my
mother did to smooth the transition, but I
no longer had to suffer the pangs of their un-
familiar habits. Still, I remember the names:
Cookie, Frankie, Johnnie, Dickie, Freddie. All
those long *e*'s echoing through the house. My
house of memory. Names thrown into gravity's forces: Cookie, Frankie, Johnnie, Dickie,
Freddie. Among others.

Among others. Isn't that
what *Company* is about? Yet there are no others. An old man lies in the dark, and what he
has for company is a Voice. Asking his own
questions. Telling his own stories. Story,
then, is the thread by which we stitch the
life together. But a story of our own choosing as we sift and sort.

THE CIRCUS TRAIN

How to be scrupulous. Inclusive. Honest. Isn't that what this is about? But when you doubt your own version, how can you not doubt the whole? And yet when you look around, when you count the people in the chemotherapy room, or in the audience at the theater, you wonder if they have the same adherence to memory, the same continuity you find in yourself. How could they, you wonder. They seem so content. So full of the moment. While poisons drip, they sink into their magazines, or chat idly with each other. The play unfolds, and they seem to take it in on its own terms. Only you, with your infernal inner voice, your hard-nosed critic, only you are locked in hypercritical analysis. Only you, making up your own story, rewriting the play, repelling the poison in favor of what you used to be. You are in the company of yourself, wrestling with the incompleteness of your memory. The conviction of that circus train.

Don't. Don't keep arguing with me, refuting what I've just said, resisting my interpretations. You always try to give others their due. You posit excuses for them. Or reasons. I don't care about the reasons. I only care that . . . that they are what I say they are. The product of my perceptions. So don't go on defending them against my stories. My stories are real. They carry themselves along the months, then years. They move slowly, horse and buggy time, and their colors do not fade. So, simply, don't. Open yourself to my version of my life—because it will eventually explain everything. Will lead to the cookie jar that holds my ashes. Open yourself to what it feels like to be burdened with memory, and insight. Or, if not insight, then critique. Commentary. So, quite simply, don't.

On the television, scenes of disaster from the East Coast's Hurricane Sandy in the fall of 2012. No one back there to worry about, so you simply stare at the screen, amazed at what nature can do. There are people there—flooded homes, lives disrupted—and yet they are, to you, abstract ideas of people. You have to remind yourself how long things take, how two months after the flood of 1972 you were pulling still-soggy insulation from between the studs of the house you grew up in. How it smelled of a river gone awry. And the long year your parents lived in a trailer parked in the driveway while they tore everything down, then built it up again, six feet of water in the first floor taking memory with it as the photos curled at the edges, came unglued. And then the house, good as new, but missing the built-in bookcases, the French doors, the friendly feel of years of living in it. The blue glass goblets rest on a new windowsill, letting the sun remind you of what water can do.

Is she heartless? All she can do is go back to her own outdated memories. Touch base with her own experience. But isn't that how memory is supposed to work? How can she know what it is to face down a grizzly, or crawl on her belly into an underground cave? She's never been close. She can pretend to know what the panic must be like, but she's always surprised herself. It's a mystery. How will she act? She has to wait and see. So there they are, people on the screen, telling their stories. And there they are, news anchors, mumbling their platitudes. And here she is, a blank slate waiting for feeling to take over. All she knows is that when those strangers go back inside their houses, they will smell the insidious scent of ruin. And their muscles will ache on into the evening after a long day of cleaning. And later, weeks later, they will sit in their new chairs and watch their old lives disappear.

All Stan says is, "It looks a bit like Halloween," and I realize I've had over seventy Halloweens, and none of them looked the same to me. When I was little, Halloween looked like what I was wearing, whatever costume I'd managed to devise from the boxes of "dress-up" clothes my mother kept in the attic. The one I remember most was when I was Johnny Appleseed and I wore a tin pot on my head, a burlap sack over my entire trunk, and carried an apple in case no one knew who I was. The problem was that that year it was cold— blustering wind and the hint of snow in the air. I didn't want to wear a coat—that would cover my sack and then definitely no one would know who I was. So that year is blue in my mind: blue lips, blue air, blue wash of plans gone south. When my boys were young, Halloween was actually more fun. I'd put on my witch's hat and put all the candy in a kettle and stir and stir as I handed it out when the doorbell rang. I'd cackle and talk in a high whiny voice. And my sons would tell me, later, that their friends had said, "Your mother is just a little bit crazy."

THE CIRCUS TRAIN

Then there were the years when only a few stray trick-or-treaters came by; we still kept a moderate bowl of candy at the ready, but we secretly dipped into our stash of sweets. Some things should go on forever, unchanging except for detail. Halloween should begin in mid-October while the sun is still sharp enough and the trees have a tinge of yellow to match—should begin with sky so blue it hurts, and air that cuts but does not slice. And then it should mellow through a week of rain, a slow predictable tapdance of rain where everything seems dismal and water pools in the folds of leaves, then drips in a steady pattern to the ground, each leaf holding a drop at its tip before finally letting it go. And then Halloween should bloom, like something resurrected—crisp and colorful. Every child should become someone else and keep that oddly magical feeling all day long. That other self should fill him up, like hearing a tenor whose voice fills every nook and cranny of the room, swells and builds and amplifies until it catches you in its downpour.

When I lie on my back in the dark, there is the steady plink of rain on the skylight to accompany me. Not steady

as in a metronome, the consistent throb of
tires on a concrete road, no, but the slightly
inconsistent steadiness of rain that falls in
little gusts, or drips from the branches in
consort with the wind. This morning, everything has the gloss of November. And yesterday—a day of fog—even the tiny down-
town was washed in gloom, the stores all
huddled in on themselves and their lights
faint, not inviting. Stan and I had to drive
on up the hill to where The Cup flashed its
red neon *Open* in order to find some color.
And even then, after we'd had our second
breakfast of the day—oatmeal and fruit for
lunch—it was only the brown sugar that
brightened the mood. Sweetened it, so that,
driving back, we could see where empty
swings drifted in the playground and two
small boats hugged the shore. Waves inched
their way up the beach, leaving a cuticle of
evidence. Then the long mist of evening, and
the night's unsteady drizzle. And this morning's nudge toward winter.

I can almost hear my father
telling me to look—there!—and then follow the arc of his finger to where the train
moves across my view. So tiny at first that
it's hard to pick it out, then impossible not

to see—so bright the cars, so clear the line of its course. But that would mean I was not in the strawberry patch, because I was alone in the strawberry patch yet here is my father's voice, his hand, nearly solid in my embryonic memory.

We held a white bath towel out the window of the Erwins' upstairs bathroom and waved and waved until the boat turned in our direction. Then we were being handed down the stairs and into the boat which had drifted right up onto the porch, and then there we were, floating over a cloud-filled lake that used to be front yards and meadows and corn fields until we reached the railroad tracks and what the grown-ups were calling high ground. In the distance, our own house seemed to rise out of water— did rise out of water—and we could walk inside it in our minds, go up the stairs, into our own rooms and our own beds with our own stuffed animals, and lie down to sleep. We were tired from the dark wash of water up to our parents' waists, and the bright light of the Erwins' living room while the men moved furniture up the stairs, and the sad sound of their voices when they couldn't save the cows in the barn and the way they whispered so we wouldn't hear, but of course we did, and we were tired of this flood that felt like what excitement was supposed to feel like, but wasn't. High ground was just the hill beyond our house, and we had nowhere to look but down and nothing to see but water where it wasn't supposed to be.

The soggy upholstery. The silt in the teacups. Even the grooves of the records, music warped and wasted. We moved to where the street took us into town. Its three steeples. Its careful plotting of avenues and boulevards and circles intersecting the grid of streets that defined our neighborhood: Hamilton, Olive, Platt, High.

How is it that you can call up the names of the streets? The avenues? Part of it, of course, is your old paper route—the weekly cycle of Sunday morning deliveries, the weekly route of Thursday evening collections, the crucial knowledge of which house wanted to cheat you, which dog wanted to bite you, which old woman wanted to talk, which one hid behind curtains. You referred to the people by address, as in "206 Hornby wasn't in again last night," or "301 Fairview never leaves a tip." The papers heavy, so heavy you began to use your old red wagon to pull them up the hill. The bundle of front sections thrown off the truck with a thud onto your front porch, then the whine of the engine as it broke open the dark. Then the weight of the wagon, growing lighter as you wound your way along your route. And in winter, you tied a box on your sled, those runners leaving their twin snakes in the snow. You are there now, ringing the doorbells and making the change, tugging the wagon over the streets of your youth—your ordinary, unembellished youth. You are caught in what you took with you when you left.

Just as you will preserve the house, with its Christmas scent of pine and cinnamon. The lights on the tree doubled, then tripled in the panes. Candy houses with peppermint-stick gutters and chocolate doors. Roll the dice. Go directly to jail. Do not pass Go. But go anyway, into that storm of recollection.

I was washing the dishes when I heard the sound. I don't know what

George or my parents were doing, but we all heard the sound. And we knew what it was, even though it was a sound none of us had heard before. We raced for the door, were heading for the tracks even before the train could fully stop. And the car it had hit had been pushed half a block up the track, tipped on its side and crumpled. Two people wandering dazed. And two lying by the side of the tracks. One stilled to nothingness. Dead in the blink of that sound. And my mother stepping into the ditch when the doctor from seven houses down asked for help with the other one. My mother pushing hard on the bleeding wounds, calm and careful, doing something she had no idea how to do. Surprising herself. Surprising us. Of all those who had rushed to the scene, my mother was the one who stepped into the mystery, felt its precarious pulse.

Where was my father, with all his Boy Scouts and first aid? I don't know. And calling up the memory will not make him appear. He's gone from the scene, as certainly as if he had never been there. Only my mother, stepping down when the doctor asked for help. And where am I in this scene? I'm standing on the edges, watching.

THE CIRCUS TRAIN

I do not know I am taking in this scene for all time. I do not know I will take it—my singular perspective—with me, out into the world, and back again, in this moment, retreating to the page. I do not know how I feel about anything, standing at the side of the tracks, unsteady on the cinders that line the railroad bed, unsteady on my feet and in my improbable brush with the newly dead.

I open the pill container with the pink plastic lid—the one they are dispensing for breast cancer month. I am sick of pink plastic this, pink plastic that, pink ribbons, pink football cleats, pink hats, pink guitars, pink against pink. I am sick of seeing what they have made of my condition. I am even sick of pink plastic flamingos, which I have always had a sort of soft spot for. Pink will not save me—all those people smug in their charity pink, running as though they could outrun fate—which, trust me, they can't.

So, she's calling up the past instead of living in the present? But she's alive back there, climbing her tree, swinging a bat, skating on the smooth ice of the vast rink that the fire department constructed each year, sitting near the bonfire to remove her skates, listening to the crack of sparks flying out into frigid air, talking on the telephone, delivering her newspapers, swimming out to the raft, lying under steaming sun, feeling the force of gravity as she pulls herself up on the water skis, roller-skating to those tinny tunes, eating hamburgers at the diner, pincurling her hair, waiting (always waiting) for his car to round the corner so they could ride off, windows down, taking in the sounds of the evening—the crickets, the steady babble of water in the creek bed—and taking in the scents of dusty July heat and the sense that this evening would go on forever, as it has. Clearly it has, since she smells it now, hears its sounds, knows what will happen next. Maroon Dodge, warm night, radio—the Everly Brothers, Elvis, some song whose words fit the darkness—and the dusk flowing past, fluid, like time itself. The back roads, they called them: Dry Run Rd., Coon Hollow Rd., Meads Creek Rd. And she will go off to college, then on into the world. And he will go into the Navy, then on into the world. And they will never see each other again, or even want to, but this night will live on in both of them as something ineradicable.

THE CIRCUS TRAIN

Or I could go another direction. The tiger cat that my aunt allowed us to adopt while my mother was away for the week. How could she? I see that now—the affront of it. But then, I only knew that Boots was ours, and that there was no way my mother could say no after one whole week of ownership. Or Tray, the dog we all chose, the one who loved to stick her head out the car window and bite at the air, nipping and nipping for the sheer, clear joy of it. Summer at its height, so we knew what she'd do when we stopped at the lake, the way she'd head for the water in such a straight line, her nose tugging her into it, her head riding and riding its surface, almost a grin. And when, finally, she was done with her swim, the shaking and shedding of water in one long chaotic shivering dance, the sun caught in the droplets until dog and rainbow were one, and were ecstasy.

I call up the names of the streets and the name of the dog and the name of the cat, and the past is the present. A present that exists alongside my view of the trees outside my window and the depths of the rain that falls, and keeps on falling. I sink into my amalgamated self and ride out the currents. What was the name of the lake? I was sure that I knew it, but I can't make its sound. It's easy to call in the others. *Come, Tray. Here, girl. Here, Boots. Here, kitty kitty.*

Who is it I bring with me as I walk out into the world? Today I need to have my glasses fixed. I managed to find the tiny screw that had come loose, but I cannot make the lens stay put as I try to tighten the nut. So I will walk through the glass door of the eye-care specialist's place and ask to have them restore me to sight. I will walk in trailing the pets and the lakes and the countries and cities I have seen: Edinburgh's wet cobblestones and the bleak highland splendor, or Brazil with its palms and its orange-tiled roofs. Ireland with its fiddles and fairs. Greek cities strung out like pearls along the bay. I will walk in and ask them to give me back the blues and greens and dismal grays of my memory, and I will walk out into the struggling sunlight of a November morning, where the ferry looms white at the dock and the gulls screech on the pilings and the rain makes syncopated drops on the windshield, makes the town turn in on itself looking for brightness and warmth.

THE CIRCUS TRAIN

Your lips are blue. Your body is shivering, your teeth chattering so hard you couldn't stop them if you wanted to. But you don't want to, you want to let your body go, let it do what it wants to do. You make a little jackhammer noise through your teeth. Uh-uh-uh-uh-uh. Uh-uh-uh-uh-uh. You jump up and down with the cold. Your bathing suit feels icy in the breeze. Your mother tries to rub you with a towel. Uh-uh-uh-uh-uh. You are in love with the way you can stay in the water until your body won't stop shaking. This is the coldest your body will ever be. Oh, it will shiver a bit before you bundle up to brave the wind, or feverishly hold itself together under the covers until your own heat can surround you, but you will never again turn blue at the gills, never again take an hour to recover from your own best fun.

You—you are moving toward the moment you can be alone, locked in the body's ultimate betrayal. You find it fascinating to realize that the flip side of yourself is an old man lying in the dark, thoughts racing through him for company. You are running toward, and Beckett was running away. From the moment his mother dropped his hand in rebuke, he was turning abandonment into abandon. You wish you knew how to abandon yourself to the moment. You did once that you can recall— riding in a boat on the Erie Canal. The evening stretched wide and on either side there were fields, the backsides of barns, fence-rows. And a heron—yes, the cliché of it!— rising from the water and seeming to float overhead, leading us on, casting its shadow in front of us. And there we were, relaxed and happy in the moment, without a hint of the past stalking us, laying its claims. Or the future either, for that matter.

If I am not careful, I will get lost in childhood. Yet it's the adult self that we lose to the humdrum of responsibility. In childhood, everything is fresh—a train drifts through the valley and there is delight.

Now it is the quotidian that I embrace, the deceptive sense that it will go on forever. The breakfasts, the loading and unloading of dishwashers, the ringing of phones, the newspaper, the mail, the exercise, the TV, the taxes. There they are: on the left side of my window, photos of my mother and father, my Aunt Margaret, my grandfather—all of them gone; on the right side, my brother, my sons, their wives, their sons. They circle me like the seasons, moving inexorably on, and then on. The only constant is William's painting of a farmhouse in France. The whiteness of the snow. Surely that farmhouse still exists. If only in the mind. If only on my wall.

Snow sifting. Silent. Filling the Vermont street with its hush, a postcard moment in the life being lived. Snow taps on the window and we walk out into its lavish new day. Snow whispers along the macadam, making little snakes of itself in the feathery wind, rising in whirls like girls dancing. It settles on the fir trees and along the bare branches of maples. It mimics the birches, is backdrop for cardinal, and jay. Snow fills your lungs, hollows them so they send breath back out, white against white.

That lake—what was its name? You know that you know the name of the lake. Something to do with food, you think. It's at the tip of your tongue, to use the cliché, but it won't tip off into the shape of its sound. You'd better settle for imperfect memory, for the sense that the train was, but wasn't where you think it was. Elusive, when what you want is certainty. What you want is simply to know that you know.

What you want is to walk each morning—oxygen 93, heart rate 126—twenty minutes of steady travel through the rooms of your house, the windows slowly brightening as daylight comes on. You want to keep that routine, then reel it out into the future, twenty minutes after twenty minutes after twenty minutes. Ad infinitum. When you know there is no such thing as infinitum. Not in human terms. And still you set one foot in front of the other.

Your footsteps overlap themselves, a figure eight, infinity sign, around and around, breathe in and out, your lungs healthy enough to weave and weave the length of the house, your eyes trained outward to where the few cars wind their way down the hill, round the corner and disappear, to where the woman from across the road will soon walk her new dog—the one she got from the pound—and where the

Mexicans who live in the house behind hers will drive off for work. Then your eyes come back, to where the hummingbird checks his schedule of flowers.

The buck—you know it was a buck because the antlers were prominent—was too fast, too fluid, for you to count the points. What does it matter? He was large, and powerful, and he leapt the fence in one flowing movement and then he was off past the side of the house. You imagine his next hurdle, over the fence at the front of the house. If you went out, you might find his hoofprints in the garden. If you went out—but you won't—maybe you could still see him, stopped in his tracks so to speak, nibbling at the neighbor's new willow. But you won't go out, won't look for him, because you still see the mystery of his being there at all, leaping your fence the way he did yesterday, and the day before.

What you took in was your tiny eastern valley with its quaint, low-slung hills. Its river slipping into its names: Cohocton, Chemung, Susquehanna, until it eventually found its way to the sea. You lived on a tributary to a tributary, and you knew enough to measure water not by its width but by the width of its bank, testimony to spring runoff and the occasional hurricane.

Today, in the fields, horses with blankets on their backs. Horses covered for the cold, when it isn't even cold. Rain, yes. But nothing like the biting wind or snow that might warrant a blanket. Back east, horses stand nose to the wind, braving the weather. But they also have barns to retreat to. Hay, and water, and the soft shifting of others in their stalls. Today, the car weaves past farms, rounds a curve, and there they are—horses, with ice-covered mountains in the distance. Ten years we've lived here, and memory-in-the-making still catches me unawares.

Once she rode horses with a modicum of abandon. Knew how to give the flank a nudge with her heel, how to lay the reins against the neck, how to dig in her knees for a gallop across the meadow. She didn't ride often, but enough to feel she knew the way a horse could give a little shiver and blow air through his nostrils, could glance over his shoulder and she should be just a bit wary. She liked the way in one moment they would nuzzle her hand and in the next try to brush her off by stepping close to a low-hanging branch. She liked nothing better than her body rocking in the saddle, swaying front to back in a dance of its own. She liked nothing better than hiking her left foot into the stirrups and swinging her right one up and over.

And Beckett? He is listening to the Voice in the dark. An abstract voice, filled with abstractions. Beckett? He understands that voice, its insistent questions. His life fills up within its acoustic range. There's a music in his mind. A symphony. Chorus of question marks. Each sharp or flat, suddenly natural. If this were *a cappella*, it would still be duet. Our thoughts hinge on his composition.

She's in love with a photo of Benjamin reading Robert Frost. What does a ten-year-old find in those poems? The rhythms and rhymes that lead farther and farther into the woods of sound. The sound that makes, as Frost would say, the sound of sense. The sense that someone who came before him had felt what he has felt and thought what he has thought. That he is not, as he would be with Beckett, alone.

Zoom in. I am alone and the sun is descending. Holding me down in its fierce need to keep me there, sifting the dirt, so alive in that moment that each leaf seems to make its own claim on the eyes, each rustle a claim on the ears. The dirt is dry, and it crumbles to powder with a touch, spills through the fingers to make a small mound to smooth and smooth until the fingers feel as though they know this one small piece of land. This one garden, this one June morning, this one sun beating down, this one tree—this could be mine forever. And forever, a word that should frighten a four-year-old, seems so very real. So solid and physical that it is there, waiting for me to call it up. *Forever.* So I write it down, setting it squarely next to the strawberry patch that will move from blossom to fruit to blossom to fruit in a circle that cannot be broken.

Okay, so my friend Diane was more daring than I was. But after the escapade with the Greek truck drivers when we were hitchhiking on a deserted highway after midnight, after she put an entire stone cannonball from Castel Sant'Angelo, the site of *Tosca*, into her purse and walked away, after she scaled the gate into the private monks' quarters at the Escorial—one movement, ripple of cat from ground to fence—well, what was I supposed to do? I felt nervous as she eyed the bell rope at Canterbury Cathedral and I pushed her in the other direction, that's what I did. Slow dissolve. I wonder what's become of Diane, whether, in some law of reversal, she has grown steadily more cautious as I have learned my own muted brand of gambling. Whether I have made curiosity a form of action. A question of degree, not kind.

We called her Leapin' Lena. Her real name was Alma Quackenbush, but we didn't know that for several years. We only knew what other kids had called her before we learned the name, and the way she walked with her wide-gaited limp, and her stringy hair and baggy clothes, and the way she would turn if we called out her name and snarl something we were too far long gone to be able to hear. We made up stories about her and we threatened younger kids with her and we kept our parents from knowing about her. We used her as our secret weapon against adulthood. We needed Leapin' Lena to have no other name, no house to go home to, certainly no one to love.

She's waiting for something to happen. She has no idea what, or when. This is the nature of her condition. She is in the dark, so to speak, lying in the dark. Alone. This will happen to her, and although others will accompany her, they will not cross the border she will cross. Is she afraid? Sometimes yes, sometimes no. Sometimes she feels that tug and it is so gentle, so inviting, that she feels she is ready. But not now. Now she feels stronger, and acceptance recedes, moves back to court denial. How can the days not go on? How can she not plan for another Halloween? another election? another five years to see how something turns out? She is waiting, she realizes, for someone to commute her sentence—and that is exactly what is not going to happen. She is waiting—oh how could she not have known this—for redemption.

Carved into the church steeple: *Redeeming the Time.* As though this cascade of bells could reverse the order of things. And maybe it can. There, the tiny poppies like spots of blood. And in the distance, the moors, with their flash of purple heather. The sky a canopy through which the larks disappear, then send their song downward. Is this not time*less*? But maybe that ancient carver had something else in mind. The sound of the bells, liberated, rising over the valley like birds lifting in unison, or pouring through the sky like molten glass. Time moving in all directions.

Quick, now, here, here is what *is*: brick clocktower against the evening sky, blue neon *Vacancy* over the motel balcony, the lit interiors of homes inviting you into rooms where the table is set, soup steaming on the stove. Christmas is coming. This is the sharp, potent flavor of the instant, not the slightly bitter aftertaste of what was. Wasn't it Eliot who wrote "What might have been and what has been / Point to one end, which is always present"? Ceaselessly present, yes, the future that never happened alongside the past that did. The ache of it. Earache, toothache, pinning you to the perpetual present even as it slips away.

JUDITH KITCHEN

Reading a letter from Henry James to William James: *This is a country of perpetual delightful commons; which ever since I have been here have been, with their heather and gorse, a glory of purple and gold.* My sons were visiting their grandfather in Baltimore when it happened—the fight that meant they were barely speaking to each other for several weeks. I remember it vividly because, in some odd way, it made me happy. The argument? Who was the better writer: Tolstoy or Dostoyevsky. The fact that they differed did not surprise me. The problem was then— and is now—that I couldn't fathom which one would choose which writer. So today I called each of them. Odd—neither one could even recall the argument, though each could speculate what he might have said then. Twenty-five years ago. So I am free to make it up, so to speak, to give them a "side" they don't even care about. I've decided to leave it alone. I know which of them is Leo, and which is Theo. I'll leave them to it. In my mind, they carry it on over a lifetime, each passionate and convinced, each one fighting for words to end all words. Both of them remember this: they are thirteen and fifteen, and we are driving through Dartmoor— stony outcrops, shy ponies, heather extending itself to a gunmetal sky. A sunflash of gorse. They are in the back seat, each tethered to his own Sony Walkman—the very instruments we've given them so they could while away some time at boring old cathedrals, or weather stop-and-start traffic between busy Midland cities. There they are, nodding their heads to a distant beat, listening to some pop song, some band whose name I will never even know, while gorse is flowering, something they really need to see. "Turn those things off," I shout at them. "Look out that window, damn you. That is gorse. That yellow plant, over there—that is gorse! How are you ever, ever going to read Thomas Hardy if you don't know what gorse is?" By now, they've both read some Hardy, and I don't know if they liked him or not. I don't know what they took away from his red earth and its moors, its lonelinesses. But I do know this: when gorse made its way into the text, both of them could call it up, having a bit of a chuckle with Tom, laughing at a mother who worries more about their memories than her own.

*F*ail *better.* But what does that mean? Should she fail in more glorious fashion, attempting to do the impossible? Should she fail more, piling up failures like firewood. And what is failure, anyway? She doesn't think she's failed at much, but then she has not attempted the impossible. Is failure just more of what has not been done? She has never traveled in Asia, or Africa, but she has not missed those places, even in prospect, so is that a failure, or simply an omission? She can make a list of things she has failed to do: go to more symphonies, learn new languages, parachute, white-water rafting, dancing the tango, lose more weight, watch less TV, be cured of cancer, have a long list of affairs, love better, love best. But how to fail better? Watch even more TV? Gain even more weight? Take on more lovers? Hard to do at this stage in her life. The answer is clear, but if she had wanted to watch less TV, surely she could have done so. Or white-water rafting. The symphony. With lovers, it's harder to say. Fail better at writing—now that is something she can imagine. Tearing down all the similes, building a more sturdy structure to hold her thoughts.

I wonder whether it would be better to probe the nature of forgetting. Of what is best left unsaid. Unthought. A condition so foreign as to feel like a new country with new foods and a language of gutteral clicks and unattainable vowels. Nasal. Or silken, like French whispered in a romantic movie. The land of the forgotten has no word for recollection. Not even a word for now.

I live in a state where you vote by mail. I mean, polling places are a thing of the past. And I miss them: those school gymnasiums, or basements in the old town hall, or annexes to the police station, filled with rows of machines, or tables where you can mark your ballot. Every year, they are dusted off and geared up, no matter the weather, in the high, flat desert of eastern Montana and the lush courtyards of Savannah, so that voting can become memory, as in "remember that year it rained so hard the roof leaked and they had to put buckets all over the place? And cold? Now that was a definition of cold." There's something communal about standing in line with people who are presumably neighbors, though you do not know them. Or seeing someone you do, and waving. There's something to say for greeting the woman who is checking your name against her register and then giving you a little sticker to put on your jacket saying "I VOTED" so that all day you are a reminder to others. There's something to be said for realizing that today is the day everyone comes together—even when they stand apart. It's two weeks before the election and the weather is turning and I've already inked in my ballot. What if I died before the election—would my vote still count? I suspect it would. So what am I waiting for? Why don't I just drop it in the mailbox and be ahead of the game? But what if something important happens in the next two weeks? Something mind-changing? I don't want to be living and filled with regret. So the envelope sits on my desk and I keep reminding myself not to forget it when the time comes and that takes me right back to those days when I couldn't forget because everyone was standing in that cold November line proving something that I now suspect we've lost.

"**M**y mistakes are my life," says Beckett. And how do you measure "mistake"? Larger than a breadbox? Tiny, the kind only you notice? Some mistakes are so grandiose that they loom over you, become your life for sure. Some mistakes happen by mistake. They take you into new territory. Not just detour, but whole new highway. You never get back to where you started so you are forced to turn them into your life. Some lives are so small there is no room for mistake. I do not want mine to have been that small. But all lives consist of what was done, what wasn't done. He must have meant more than that. But then, it's Beckett. So maybe not.

Your life is one vast swirl of memory, and you want to let it ferment and distill like a good Scotch whiskey. And just like that—there it is—the Talisker distillery on the Isle of Skye, white against the green hillside, white above the black waters of Loch Harport. There it is with the rough-hewn doorway and the spidery crack in the cinderblock. Barrel upon wooden barrel stored in a warehouse with the faint, sweet smell of liquor—the 2% that evaporates, the part they call the "angels' share." The vocabulary, not exactly new to you, but rarefied now, confined to the process at hand: malting, mashing, fermentation, distillation, maturation. The fine-tuned order of it all. You would like to pour yourself a glass. The taste of peat. A dusky fire, banked and then rekindled. The past, condensed in this one moment as you pull into the parking lot.

JUDITH KITCHEN

Fields of barley. Many years have passed, and there you are, the two of you, taking the B road to Carbost, then on to Kyleakin where you will wind your way down through the highlands to Glencoe, which has its own dark memories, its own past to distill.

So, both of you remember the woman at the blackhouse, the one who told you your ancestors were "good people," the one who seemed to think that 1746 was just last year. Or at least, the memory of the loss at Culloden had persisted so that she spoke in almost-present tense. "We was just seventeen miles from London and we turned around," she says. "We could've smashed them and now they've smashed us and we've lost our Prince Charlie." Her memory now a part of our memory, and our memory about to take its inevitable branches as our lives, as lives do, diverge. I mean, we share that day and we share our lives, but most certainly that day means something different to each of us. The house—with its lack of a chimney—blackened with use. Its tiny rooms that had held crofters until time ran out and they were "cleared." The one tiny room used only for birthings, and the laying out of the dead. Stan saying, "it must have been empty so much of the time," and the woman replying, "No, it was almost always in use." Our assumptions about what it is to live suddenly come face-to-face with history. The crofters must have had such different thoughts from ours. Different forms of denial and acceptance. That is, if they had time for thought as they stoked the fire and fetched the water and sheared the sheep and tended the land and worried about the distant landlord and sang of their bonnie Prince Charlie.

See? I know I saw that blackhouse. Wandered its two tiny rooms and touched its walls and listened to the woman's ferocious sense of the past. But the multi-colored circus train?

We're sitting at the dinner table when suddenly Ian, who is three, says, "I have something to tell you." Ian never says much, just sits back and enjoys the world, so we all become quiet to listen. He tells us a long, involved story about being in Utah and making snowballs, then stops abruptly, "Okay, guys?" We laugh, but later we find it unnerving. His story happened, yes—but when he was tiny, long before he could talk.

JUDITH KITCHEN

So this is pre-verbal memory, a moment embedded as image, waiting for words.

Okay guys? Suddenly he is one of us. Already looking backward. Summing up, making of, reminiscing about, thinking through.

You never see yourself tripping down the stairs in black patent-leather sandals and lacy collars, or playing dolls with other girls. You see yourself up in the tallest branches of the tree, in brown leather Oxfords—the only shoes your mother will buy you, skinning the cat on the closet rail, or hanging upside down from the jungle gym, or riding your bike, or poking a stick into the river to test its depth, or pretending you are riding ponies over the moors—always a boy. You see yourself a tomboy and the neighbors see you as a tomboy and you are proud of it. But you are barred from playing Little League ball, and you are angry. You will prove something to them all. You will prove that you can do anything a boy can do. Better. Your own fierce feminism is born not of concession, but of oiling your

mitt and showing you could hit grounders
with the best of them.

Messi flows down the pitch
in his light blue shirt, moving like a river
bound for its mouth. A flash of his boot
and the ball arcs into the air, holds itself in
still-motion at the apex, then hurtles into
the net. A flash of his boot and he's done it
again! Messi ducks and twists and weaves in
and out, effortless on the field. Fluent in his
dark blue and maroon, he pours like honey.
This is past perfection.

We've turned the clocks
back, so dark comes early and time is prob-
lematic. I am lying on my back in the half-
light of late afternoon. The rain is stuttering
on the roof, making its half-hearted attempt
at becoming full-blown storm, or else stop-
ping altogether. It's hard to tell which. It is
November and rain is ubiquitous. My winter
journal will be filled with the isolation of
rain, the isolating fact of rain. I am lying
on my back and thinking of nothing. We've
turned the clocks back so I am already looking forward to turning them forward. Losing
an hour to gain sunlight again.

JUDITH KITCHEN

How do you delineate long summer nights where the hum of the city—its horns and sirens and streaming bright lights—was a turning toward one form of failure? The Bronx—just two words to call up his name and the heft of his voice. No way to memorize the life you did not live. The ship that did not sail. While the one that did took you to Edinburgh and, from there, to here. Here and now. This particular day, where to look out the window is to see high branches whirling in a frenzy of wind. Is to hear the steady whine of what might have been.

Odd how the body seems to carry the years on its back. Piled up, one upon another, an increasing heaviness. Yet some people carry theirs lightly. Maybe they are the ones who are good at forgetting. Each day comes new, like fresh-ground pepper perking up the palate. They go out into it open to whatever it brings. But I am burdened with memory, its unerring sense of itself, so the new days must be measured against the old. The remembered. I'd like to borrow from Robert Frost and "disremember." Active forgetting. I'd get rid of the day you turned and walked away. I'd get rid of hurt and annoyance and boredom. Who should have to recall the days of sitting on the front porch watching small children pedaling by on tricycles? Day after day. A water torture of tricycles. And my own sons among them, daily responsibility trickling through the hourglass and eating up time. Time when I might have been thinking, or doing, or at the very least wondering. Time I cannot bring back even as I spend months of it in recollection.

Briefly, you felt what nature had in store: a shutting down, lungs heavy with a liquid of their own making, the in and out of breath until you drift, dizzy, float into nothingness. Briefly, you surrendered. And then the drug kicked in with its truck-load of weight, hit you broadside and turned you into gelatin. You became nothing but the drug; you turned on its spindle.

Don't talk about patience. Nature's slow, sweet patience. Think, instead, of its opposite: hurricanes, hail-storms, volcanic eruptions. Things that change the landscape. You look up and it's altered. That whirr of the hummingbird which, magnified, becomes the tornado's drone. That brushfire of wind. Happenstance of flood.

On this morning's walk I turned around at the fireplace and faced the pile on what we call the kitchen table but where we mostly never eat: eleven books, old newspapers, junk mail, some empty plastic bags, plastic bags with something in them, a yellow file folder, one vase of old carnations (in fair shape), another vase of new tulips (purple, drooping), a paper bag that once held a prescription from Safeway, several scarves, and, of course, my wig. The reason for the wig being on the table is that I have a strong suspicion bordering on belief that hair grows faster out in the open than it does under a wig. I can't prove this theory because I don't have two heads, and I'm unwilling to shave off what hair I do have to start the experiment over again. Anyway, while I was staring at the table—or rather, the lack of table—out of the corner of my eye I saw the crow. That is, I thought it was a crow, staring in at me through the sliding glass doors to the deck. "That's one bold bird," I thought, and, "What's he eating?" before I realized that it was the black metal crow we bought some years ago, the one with a bead in its beak. Damn, I thought, that crow has really weathered the weather better than I have.

One, two, three, four, five, six, seven, eight. One, two . . . I walk to an eight-count, around and around, looking out into the day. Today there is sun somehow finding its way underneath the clouds so that they look as though a spotlight were shining up, lighting them from beneath. They glow—gray to white to pink—but I know that this is temporary. In a minute or two, they will become ordinary clouds. And the day will make its way into the bank of days as either ordinary or not, depending. Today is election day, so it's likely to be inscribed in memory simply because it will be momentous, one way or another. We measure time in four-year increments, election to election, what happened when, who was president when, where we were when . . . and that's the way we know how old we are, when we remember vividly Kennedy's assassination, Nixon's resignation, 9/11. My grandchildren were all born after that day in 2001 when the towers fell, taking our innocence with them. What will they remember? Today?

JUDITH KITCHEN

Possibly, but I'm betting they will measure time by larger, more amazing events. Still, I see myself one November night sitting in a darkened movie theater in Edinburgh. On the screen, scratched into the film in shaky capital letters, PRESIDENT KENNEDY ASSASSINATED IN U.S. We waited, all of us, for the punch line to appear. And when it didn't, and didn't, an intake of breath. In unison. A sudden recognition that this had gone beyond the timing for a joke. Was real. Though how could we comprehend it? Should we leave? But what would we do? And, being Scots now in practice as well as spirit, we stayed. We had paid. So we sat through Pinter's *The Caretaker* and emerged into the Edinburgh night to see flags streaming at half-mast, an outpouring of flags from every building. Unreal, or so it seemed then, and so it seems now, fifty years later.

I was twenty-two. What did I know? I knew that my president had been shot, and that I was far away from home, and that I could not take heart from shared experience. On 9/11, I called my brother on the West Coast, I talked to my students, to colleagues, to my sons, to my husband, and

62

although none of it made sense, we made its non-sense together. I was twenty-two, and I felt inescapably alone. Some time later, my mother told the story of how she wanted my grandmother to rest a bit during the day while she herself was away at work. So she asked my grandmother to take notes during a particular soap opera. That night, when my mother returned, she found a note pinned to my grandmother's apron: *Laura thinks Peter is seeing Amy, Sam visited Ellen, President Kennedy shot, Dorothy and Janice meet for lunch.* No distinction between fact and fiction. Her mind a wonderful mix of illusion and reality. A Pinter mind, while I was watching Pinter three thousand miles to the east in an entirely different time zone so that, for me, he will always die in the evening, while for most people, it was 2:00 p.m. and the plaza was a blaze of sunlight caught on the hood of the car. A fleeting glint in a window that will change our history.

$\qquad$

You wobble as you walk, a little bit like a drunk. The irony is that now you cannot drink. It interferes with too many medicines, the ones you dole out into the container, six for each morning. Then you have to remember the other four that you take at other times of the day. And that says nothing of the two shots you have each month. Those other shots you gave yourself, your stomach laid bare, were nothing compared to the continual drip of chemotherapy that clouded your months, your years. So start at the toes, where neuropathy starts. Or else start with the hair that doesn't grow, will not grow fast enough for you to forget. Start anywhere, because everything has been affected. Begin with your mind, where you are most alive, and the way it loses whole words, whole names for things you know you know. As though your whole life were disappearing, word by word, drip by steady drip. Words like *ruse*, or *palate*, or *benign*. That childhood lake where your chattering teeth made their jackhammer sound.

T here's this: we're riding in an old Chevette, so low to the ground it gets stuck on speed bumps, and here we are crossing a rickety one-lane wooden bridge somewhere deep in the Green Mountains of Massachusetts. I mean deep, even in such defined territory. We're lost, or almost lost, and the bridge has gaping holes in it and the tires are so small. The autumn woods are still a faded yellow, and somewhere around

THE CIRCUS TRAIN

here is an abandoned cemetery. I want to find it so I can imagine how it looks in winter. Somewhere near here I hope to learn the rules of risk.

There you are: two of you riding the merry-go-round—the one that later burned down, so your horses were gone forever. Two of you, too old for this, but there you are, up and then down, the cracked paint smoothed by thousands of hands, your horse with its one odd eye. And there he is, reaching for the brass ring that always eludes him. And there it is, the music that seems a hundred years old, and maybe it is. It has coiled its way around a million riders over the years, a tinny waltz, ethereal and yet solid as oak. Run your fingers over the mane—the deep indentation in wood, wood that swirls and dips to the cadence of the song. There they are, the two of you, at the cusp of love. And yet he goes down when you go up, so you have to catch each other's eye somewhere in the middle. And the day stretches out, the sun roars down and soon you will leave. But for now, let them hover on the brink. Let your skirt billow in the circular breeze and the horse cast its wild eye backwards.

JUDITH KITCHEN

Okay, so I'm not sure about some things, but others are decidedly crisp and clear. Like apples in October. You bite in and taste the summer running down. I can will up that horse and his manic eye, will up my feelings of discontent. Remember? The day smoothed itself out, like a sheet pulled up to the chin. Smoothed itself out, then wrinkled again, so that all that was left of our leaving was my wish to be circling and circling.

And this: the geese pecking away at the windows in Grasmere. Tap. Tap, tap. The ominous Morse code of it.

One lone cardinal. A flash of brilliance against the snow, then gone, leaving his two-tone note behind. *Not here. Not here.* Now, brilliance is reserved for the brief appearance of a Steller's jay, blue commotion on the madrona. Or the fluorescent sheen where crows hold sway, preening on the overhead wires. Where the grating *caw, caw, caw* becomes so raucous, so chaotic, that you want to shut it down, run out and wave your arms and shout—and now you know why the original scarecrow was invented.

THE CIRCUS TRAIN

Never mind saving the corn. Save your ears, your sane, sensible ears. So the cardinal calls in memory, flits from branch to branch. And you search for his mate—her green-tinged blush—but she's nowhere in sight. Is he calling to her? You think not. You think he's calling for the sheer sake of song, for the way it can fill up the branches and pierce the frigid air. And the air? It holds each sound in its cupped hands, releases it to the bright winter sky. And the sky? It's been some time since you've seen a sky that blue, that cold. That capable of framing the tree with its one spot of flame.

Odd how we relive not only scenes, but the camera-flash moments in which everything stops and we take notice of what will later become description. Or else circumstance, held in abeyance until the eye can take in and make sense of. Odd how these moments take up no time at all as we relive them, yet took so long back then, living through them. It's as though we have a fast-forward mode. Hold them there—mother, father, brother, apricot tree, merry-go-round—then place them in a centrifuge. The spinning years falling past each other in a tumble of time. The precipitate falling like snow, little flakes of the self that settle as sediment in the bottom of the glass.

"**M**ight not the voice be improved? Made more companionable. Say changing now for some time past though no tense in the dark in that dim mind." The page has been turned down, dog-eared years ago, though I do not remember the finger and thumb at the corner. What, back then, made me think I would need it now? What tenseless time did I imagine?

There are always the firsts— the first time for anything much more vivid than its cousins who follow and fade. The first time you went skating, the ice—so fast and furious—slipping out from under you. The first time you went to a movie—*Bambi*— and how sad it seemed at the end, the fawn bounding at the bottom of the credits, the doe alive and leaping. The feel of the shiny flute in your hands, your fingers hovering over the holes, the current of silver notes as your breath crossed the embouchure. First train ride, first plane ride, first steamship heading into open sea. The first faint throb of your heart, first kiss, first sex (though

you'll keep that private right up to the end).
First marriage, first childbirth, first divorce.
You could sum up a life in those six words,
though they'd leave out the groundswell of
detail. They'd leave out yesterday and today.
You know they'd leave out tomorrow.

But tomorrow comes with
news of remission, though they don't really
call it remission. Just a cessation. A guess
that the drugs must be working, for now.
A mystery they can't explain. You'll take it,
though, the time redeemed. Time handed
back to make something of, though what
can you do but waste it?

Under your feet, the ground
swells and buckles. You can no longer han-
dle even the slightest depression. Under your
compromised feet, ground is your enemy.
Over your head, the intermittent call of
birds. This is all of nature you have seen. But
come to think of it, what else is there but the
big adventure? The kind that requires pitons
and carabiners, boots, tents, or else paddles,
life jackets. How natural is that? You prefer
the gentle walk into what appears, at first
sight, to be green, but becomes, up close,

speckled, dappled, stippled—amalgam of motion and stillness.

Still life. Your eyes are slits. The yard silent. Rare words rolling off your tongue in endless permutations: *lambshanks, scrimshaw, gandy-dancer.* And things—the plethora of things. They declare themselves: knuckles and ankle socks, spiders and spatulas. Paper bags, ocelots, Band-Aids, menorahs. Jazz bands; cupcakes; cufflinks; curbstones. Sheep dogs. Snail trails. Feeding troughs, turntables, dust jackets, dictators. Folding chairs, holding pens, inkstains, and earrings. Roller skates, home plate, briefcase, and barn owl. Popcorn; handlebar; fishing pole; fiddle. Crabcake; snowbank; branding iron; headlight. Applesauce. Skyscraper. Sunscreen. Cellphone. Seashell smoothed by the incessant sea. You could go on naming this world as long as there is still life in you.

No name for the muffled sound of chronic rain. For the smell of new-mown hay, or the pinwheel of sun that splays itself on the horizon. No name for the delicate brand of trust that fills the waiting room, or the quiet cloud where poisons drip in artificial light. And what *would* you call the moment before the moment the cell divides?

I am holding my mother's hand as we walk down River Road to visit the Harrs. Mr. and Mrs. Harr are always glad to see me and they offer me hard candies from the clear glass bowl on their coffee table. They seem interminably old to me, but probably are really only hovering in their fifties. They seem old because the house smells old, and I tell my mother I don't want to go because I don't like the smell and she explains that they enjoy it so much that we owe it to them to hold our noses and be nice. I say it's the smell—and it is—but it's also Johnny. Johnny Harr is Mr. Harr's brother who was gassed in World War I. I don't know what that means, but now we're in World War II and so it seems as though it's something that keeps happening, and I don't want anybody I know to be gassed and come home to live with his brother. Johnny walks with a limp, but the worst thing about him is the way he tries to talk, but can't. Instead, he makes loud wailing sounds that the Harrs pretend to understand, but really they couldn't possibly make sense of the trail of vowels that seem to begin deep in Johnny Harr's throat and then escape into the air. I am afraid of Johnny, but my mother says he wouldn't hurt a flea, whatever that means. *Aiiiii, ooooooh, waaaah, eeeee.* Johnny tries to talk to me, but I move closer to my mother on the couch to where my hip touches hers and I suck hard on the peppermint, as though it could make everything smell better.

When we moved west, we took on new vocabulary. No longer exotic, the words *peninsula, strait, ferry, conversion zone, rain shadow,* and *orca* have made their way into our daily rounds. And words such as *lake effect, blizzard, leaf peepers, cardinal* have receded into memory—back there, we say, as we drive between lodgepole pines. When we go back to visit, the trees look so small, so close to the ground, with spreading branches that tangle the air.

On our way home the plane will bank and the lights of Seattle will stretch along Puget Sound, and our hearts will quicken with this new landscape we've decided to make our own. We'll merge onto

THE CIRCUS TRAIN

I-5, then off for the ferry, bright light on the water as we move into the dark of our drive. Up Kitsap Peninsula, over the Hood Canal Bridge—a floating bridge—and then on north, skirting the Sound to where it opens to the Strait of Juan de Fuca. We're home, we say, as the lights of our tiny town appear in the distance, the smoke from the paper mill rising, backlit, into the night. We're home, we think, because that is where we keep the past in the form of photographs, trinkets, the comfortable furniture that takes our bodies in. The words we know now as shorthand for where we will go, what we will do—*the fort, Hudson Point, Chetzemoka, Uptown, The Rose.*

Sun! Sunlight on water. A dazzle of sun, and the air with its late-autumn chill. I fit my scarf around my neck. I fit my wig onto my head. I am ready to be public. Someday soon I will have to test the waters, go without the wig and see what happens. My hair is growing, but it's so sparse. If I run my hand over it, it's soft, like sifting sand, no, finer than that—sifting silt. A dandelion's fluff. In summer the wig will be so hot. I want to be used to myself before then, to be used to how large my face appears under my lack of hair, used to this moon in the mirror, exposed in the excessive glare.

Beckett lies in the dark and fits his mood to his point of view. It becomes him. And I sit in this blinding light thinking how I simply want time—time to complete this remembrance of things present. This recollection of things to come.

Your life is one vast eddy. Your hair flies out. You have the windows wound down and the summer air deepens into evening. The car rounds the bend and the radio carries you on, into the woods on either side. You move straight into the wind. Into the song, with its static stutter. Your hair flies out. The skates make a whisper on the clean white ice and the pond is deserted, except for you and a friend, both of you sweeping in, and then out, swiveling until you are moving backward—a centripetal pull—your hair whipping into your face. Your hair flies out like wind itself as the swing makes its arc up, and then back, your knees pumping it forward, up and out, higher and higher as you poise for flight, for

THE CIRCUS TRAIN

letting your hands leave the chains and hurtling yourself through sky before your knees bend to absorb the shock of being back in your body again. You're wearing your strawberry skirt and a clean white blouse and the horse casts its wild eye backwards. Your hair flies out as though it could replicate your heart, this day, this one day when the two of you have been released from time, have come here to replay a youthful love you never had, but clearly—now—you wish for.

In the strawberry patch I am a part of the world. Not apart, the way I often feel, but a portion of the whole. If I look up, there is the upstairs window. I can imagine myself inside, see my room with its soft green bedspread and the smell of folded sunshine in the sheets. Its dollhouse waiting for me to move the people in and out, place them on the tiny chairs or put them to bed. But mostly I want to be out here where I place myself at the center. I will reach out my hand for another hard clump, and I will take the clod between my fingers and begin to crumble it, slowly, watching it turn into a stream, a waterfall that flows into itself making a perfect cone in front of me and the dirt will spread out like silk, or what I think silk must be like.

Is this all there is? This circus train of thought that sifts through the fingers and becomes the color of the earth that holds it?

In Rio, the women wind white scarves around their heads, trail white skirts as they wade into the water. Stroke of midnight, New Year's Eve, and the frenzied sound of drums beating, beating, a throb on the sand. The bodies twisting, dancing barefoot on the sand. The women with their tiny boats—each one holding a trinket, a mirror, a comb, a candle—walking into the sea. Setting them free to float out into Guanabara Bay, offerings to Yemanja, queen of the sea, goddess of oceans, lover who calls the fishermen home. In each mirror the candle is repeated, a wavering sea of light so the goddess will remember. So she will not tug at the feet of children or rise up in angry storms to claim her beautiful men. So she will settle in the deep, glancing at herself in the mirror and combing and combing her mantle of hair. And we—we are onlookers, walking the sand with our empty hands. Who will save us? Where is our *orisha*, we of little faith? How will we keep this night with its rhythms that work their way into the heart and send it beating, faster and faster, a whirlwind of sound? How will we keep our children safe? We have seen men drown in the pounding surf, and we know that elevators plummet, and high-rises burn. We know the sun batters the sidewalks and each day's newscast counts the dead of dehydration.

Faith. Leap of.

My sons don't remember, or not much. Well, of course they do, but the memories seem so narrow. Vague. Matthew remembers a scrap of song, and William remembers standing on the balcony of the hotel in Novo Friburgo and thinking that the jungle was right there, before him, and how imperative it was. You could attribute this to how young they were, but now, as men, they plead their lack of memory as the reason for a number of omissions. William always blinks, then says, "I have a bad memory." I want him to want to remember more. Matthew uses forgetfulness more as a reluctance to make definitive plans. And Stan seems to forget the instant he's heard, so the question is asked again. Sometimes three times. "I was just checking," he maintains. Even my brother claims to have forgotten. I do not understand. Who wouldn't want to hold on to what could so easily pour through the fingers and get away? I move toward my memories, drawn to the iron filings of my past.

Olha, Natalia. Look at us. The boys have learned the words for getting attention. They climb the jungle gym—*olha*—or kick the soccer ball—*olha*. Look at them as they negotiate this new terrain, this land where vultures ride the thermals and something insidious rides underneath the surface. *Olha.* Because to listen is to hear the jungle growing and to touch is to hold the ominous in your hand. *Olha*, because the sun defines the panorama, makes even poverty look bright.

Messi shoots—and misses. "Well, we know he's human," says the sportscaster. So we measure humanity by mistake? Or failure? Eighty seconds later, he scores. "Don't tell me about statistics," the announcer shouts. "There *are* no statistics for someone who can balance a balloon in a wind tunnel." There are no statistics—the doctor reminds me—but still the vocabulary: law of averages, random variable, axioms of probability, base-rate fallacy, double-blind. Not to mention appeal to ignorance and margin of error.

Beckett turns out the light and turns to himself. "A voice in the first person singular. Murmuring now and then, Yes I remember."

Yes, and then yes, and yes, so much to remember. There's no explanation why she mostly remembers the blossoms drifting like snowflakes. Her solitude and her swift, bare feet.

And why she persists in third person. The berries are not there—not yet—are not even hard green nibs at the tip of their stems. But she knows that later they will appear, turn a faint pink, then ripen to red. But never, not once, does she call up the taste, though clearly she knows its heart-shaped sweetness.

Ah-ha—things are looking up. I mean, I'm looking up. That is, back there, who I used to be is, maybe, looking up toward the far hill and, part way up, the railroad tracks crossing the landscape. A tiny speck of color trails its way across the scene, flickering through the trees then out into the open—red and green and orange and baby blue and yellow. Almost a child's toy, but it can't be, because there it is, in Technicolor, crossing the countryside. And I stand there, nearly five years old, wearing my red-and-white-striped overalls as I stare and stare at the distant spot where my father's finger points. I try so hard to call up the detail, intact, but instead there is conjecture. And no one to confirm.

He held my hand across the table and that will never be enough. It's as simple as that. So I make for myself a future in which it *is* enough and we go forward from that moment on. Or maybe that should be past tense—we went forward from that moment on. The time is coming when tense will not matter. What has been will be what is. Will forever be. And she and I and you and we and even they have merged into one, and that one will exist only on the page. What we want is to get it all down because we fret about the meaning of things, as though things in our lives have actual meaning when we know they just happen, at random, and then we force them into meaning because we want to hold on. Because the body is compelled, breath by inevitable breath, to keep on going—inhale, exhale—making its meanings out of thin air. We care whether our lives are what we think they might have been, whether we have been a little of who we hoped to be. Face it, don't we—all of us—really want to know whether that train moved across the page in reality or in dream?

The images resolve to collage. To masterpiece of memory. But I also remember what I didn't do or see, didn't think or cause. Is this not part of the equation? A life without much in the way of drama. Or risk. A simple life in which the days mount their own defense.

JUDITH KITCHEN

"As then there was no then so there is none now."

The sound of the ponies penetrates the early-morning darkness. Here they come, we think, our waking minds shifting to what we know: the way they are set loose at the top of the hill to make their own way down to pasture. Here they come from the Gap of Dunloe to this wide field below us. Wild joy as they move in unison. "Remember the ponies at the Gap of Dunloe?" In each of us sound rises first, their hooves an insurgence on the road and sometimes a faint whinny. Then the sight of what we never actually saw—the restless sea of their glistening backs and the grins on their faces.

Gap of Dunloe, Winding Stair Gap, gap in memory, gaping hole. The words resolve to image. They build in the brain, then blossom in their blues and greens and reds. Even the absent ones—the ones we've only seen through someone else's eyes—take on imagined color. And still we move within what we think we know we know.

THE CIRCUS TRAIN

First, a watery sob in the distance. *Whooo-oooo.* Then the piercing wail as the train flies through the crossing. You rush to the back yard and stand beside the fence, waiting for it to hurtle past. You wave, and sometimes, if he sees you, the engineer waves back. But he's not the one you're looking for. He sees the world unfolding. No, you want the cabooseman. You count on him to wait for you—there in his familiar red cabin. Count on him to wave you back into your life as his world plays catch up, what he sees disappearing before his eyes. Flashback. So long, farewell. These days you drum your fingers on the steering wheel as you sit at the barrier, looking up the tracks, waiting for the train to end. Surprising you every time with its missing punctuation mark.

George and I have ordered Dick Tracy Secret Decoder rings. We know what will happen—they will arrive and they will be cheap and tawdry. But still, we anticipate them, wait every day for the mail, wait to open the package and begin sending each other our secret messages. How easy it is to be dated by two simple words: Dick Tracy. Who, now, knows who he was? Is, since it's a mystery how characters seem to live on in present tense. And words, also, resist their sure demise. *Jukebox*: It used to be an essential and now it's the source of nostalgia. Elvis belting out his gospel songs, voice like sandpaper smoothing wood. Neon, the glowing box presided over the diner, and we crowded around it, hips swaying, hoping one arm would brush against *his* arm, that boy with the ducktail haircut, the swaggering buckle of his belt. *Bonfire*: The hiss of it, long into the night. The family caught in its stammering glow, faces lit then dark then lit as though they might be caught unawares. Marshmallows turning brown in the flame. Careful, they can flare in an instant, then taste of ash. *Metastasis*: When she told me, I was in the QFC parking lot where cellphone reception is notoriously bad. And so I heard the words, but then lost the connection, and there I was, with metastasized breast cancer and nothing to do but drive home with the groceries. What more was there to say? *Soccer*: The word conjures so many games I have watched—World Cup, UEFA, La Liga, MLS. My sons on the field and the slant light of October turning it eerily bright with what might be. They glide beneath glossy trees, residing in their fluent bodies, no more mine than they ever were. *Ritual*: Ringing the changes. Each progression peals over the valley, variant of a variant, note after note, century after century. Thousands of forgotten people have stood in this place where I stand. The supple bells lift in harmony, pour through the sky.

Oh, be real. Or at least ordinary. *Bicycle*: Mine was a fat-wheeled green Schwinn, bought with a year's allowance and my father relenting to pay the rest. It was my ticket to freedom, moving through town under a canopy of maples. Green, then red, then bare, then lighter green, then the little whirlybird seeds we split and placed on our noses. *Boredom*: I don't remember being bored, though I do remember long stretches of time when I wished myself elsewhere. The endless wait in the appropriately named waiting rooms. My grandmother's nonstop review of her week. Boredom came later, with motherhood—with nothing to do but be there. *Barefoot*: That's better, carpet of grass so your feet sank into the earth. Sand so hot you hopped from one foot to the other, a juggle of toes, then raced for water. *Radio*: "Hi-Yo Silver," the galloping horses of yesteryear; "Our Miss Brooks" with its can of laughter; the strange dull news as my father sat through lunchtime listening to the Army-McCarthy hearings. *School*: Blackboards; erasers that you took outside and clapped together releasing a telltale haze on the playground; desks bolted down in their tight, straight rows; folding your hands in front of you, trying so hard not to talk; the walk home under maples. *Bereft*: Because isn't it ubiquitous—the missing, the loss, erasers and Tonto and waiting rooms, relegated to the past? A place you will enter soon enough.

Today the wind is bitter and I have no intention of going out. I'll watch it all from inside, seen piecemeal, through venetian blinds: the frantic needles of pines overhead, deer hunkered down to shelter near the fence. The foghorn. I will need to imagine the waves whipped to a fury of whitecaps down near the lighthouse. I can see them so clearly they might as well be memory. Behind me the digital clock turning and turning . . . chip . . . chip . . . chip . . . chip . . . a rhythmic trail of seconds. Pulse of time, feeding on itself. The hardcore present.

Beckett listens in the dark. The voice is full of questions; they punctuate the future. Beckett listens and notes his listening, notes the darkness and frames it—a portal, a doorway where light seeps underneath, delineating its dimensions. He lies on his back and listens until the clock becomes the darkness and darkness has become the repetition of night. I will lie on my back and placate him with answers. Today I will make one word follow another, like footsteps in snow forging a trail for someone to follow. A man lying in bed listening to a voice in his head, or a woman who wants, and then keeps on wanting, as if she could fill up the page with desire and life would not go on without her.

I stand on the moor, facing my future, listening to a wind that sweeps in without compassion. I will stand there forever. I stand on the stern of the ferry, facing the shore we've just left, listening to a wind that has crossed the ocean. I will stand there forever.

Benjamin loves Poe's "The Raven." He tells his mother that the opening of the poem "just fills you up." Isn't that how reading should work? That you become filled, however briefly, with another person's way of being in the world. Only this. And nothing more.

"The way a crow / shook down on me / the dust of snow / from a hemlock tree" and you are standing there with Frost as the featherweight of white drifts down scattering brilliance on his shoulder. It's a small crow, eastern variety, the kind that clack their way along the rows of corn. Black against white, he settles down with an unfailing touch—a lightness on the branch, a shape that sweeps in from the woods then returns to its shadows. Not one of these large western versions, messy and irritable, noisy convocation in the trees behind the house. These crows do not produce a dusting of anything, and besides, the snow here is heavy and wet, weighted with incongruity. It comes in clumps and clusters. But that moment—no more than a second's duration—when snow shakes loose at the brush of a wing, that moment is lodged in the heart so that the words *crow, dust, hemlock* call up the winter afternoons of childhood: the stillness, the faint whistle of wind, the metallic taste of icicles clutched in soggy mittens, the freezeframe persistence of time as it carries the captive past forward.

THE CIRCUS TRAIN

Thanksgiving. William is standing again on the balcony in Novo Friburgo, so intent on having us see what he saw, hear what he heard, that we can almost listen to the jungle growing. "It was so amazing," he says, and his eyes are so fierce, that blue—*morpho* blue—of his boyhood. He doesn't know what else to say—only the fact that he wanted to jump over the railing and be swallowed.

You never see yourself except wrong-way in the mirror. The crooked smile on the wrong side of your face. That's why you hate having your picture taken. You don't recognize yourself; that is not the person who holds your thoughts, who lives your inner life. That person walks out in the world with the rest of the crowd, and you pass her in the street without detection. Who *do* you recognize, since your sons surprise you, your brother and husband and, in retrospect, your parents? Those you think you think you know. So now you wonder. Beckett, yes, but also Joyce and Frost. They speak to you. But not for you. Admit it, Woolf is just too predictable. Your thoughts overlap. Of course there are others and you could sort and name them, but really, you've lost interest. Wait. Edna O'Brien. Though she is only who you want to be. Wanted to be, past tense, because her thoughts belong to a much younger woman. Odd how characters live on, decade after decade, always the age they used to be, while you age in the mirror. An elderly (you are reluctant to say old) woman peers back, and her issues are no longer their issues. They seem so young, so intense, their futures so uncertain. Clearly, she has outlived them. She wants to tell them that things will work out or they won't, and that either way it will have been a life. That the alternative is often just as interesting as what you thought you wanted. But they wouldn't listen, locked as they are between the blue or green or black covers of their books. Locked, as they are, in the present tense of the author who wrote them.

"To let in and shut out the dark."

There it is on the computer: our apartment building on Praça Pio XI. The shutters where light became the color of water as it entered the room. The open windows that carried the restless sounds of the night. The open darkness when electricity failed and the whole *praça* grew suddenly mute. See—there's our old balcony, just visible, as we click on the arrows that whirl us through time. Though there is no "us" since the boys have long since left the playground and the "we" has turned into a "he" and an "I." I can't decide where we lived: this half-familiar building on the screen or that distant ghost where the little canary stirs in its fidgety cage. Now there's a new "we" who never lived there at all.

To step up a curb. To move from the street to the sidewalk by picking up one foot and placing it on the curb. To be able to make the leg bend, then hold. To take the body from one plane to the next. To take the air into the lungs, to find the center of gravity, to hoist the body into the air, to breathe the body onto the curb.

Do not go gentle. But what does that mean? "She fought hard to the very end," people say, as though that carries the tincture of virtue. I surprise myself at my lack of rage. This does not seem in character, but there it is. The body eases itself into the water. It learns by going. Sometimes I feel as I did when I was learning to type, the *chippa-chippa-da* of the keys lulling me—*The quick brown fox jumps over the lazy dog*—over and over, jumping his way across the page. Or differential equations, the methodical calculus that calmed me with its promise of proof. Or that long first month after his birth when I propped myself up in bed and held Matthew on my shoulder during the night, his little body restless so that I dozed and woke and dozed in a dreamy stupor. Or the rhythmic smack of waves against the dock, the faint, far voices of children at play. Or the way I could sink into a book—so deep that even noise would fade and I would find myself elsewhere, walking the moors or fishing the Big Blackfoot or heading to the lighthouse, and it took extreme effort to call myself back. Lying on my back in the dark. That, too.

This morning I saw robins in the bush outside my window. They were fretting in the cold, and I worried about them. They ruffled their feathers and tossed their beaks and looked decidedly as though they wanted April. I want April, too. But I'm stuck inside, and this watery scene will have to do—for the time being. I like the phrase "for the time being." Time being what it is, I move through it as if I were swimming. Stroking my way through the minutes and hours. I know I don't appear that way— appear resolute, as though I know what I'm doing at all times. I like the phrase "at all times" as though each minute were, some- how, equal. As though they added to each other in steady increments and you could dip in and pull one out and it would stand for all the rest. But I know that all times are not equal, that sometimes you don't notice its passage and sometimes you have time on your hands. I like the phrase "time on your hands" when you can actively hold it and feel its weight. It's heavier than you might think, and that's when time hangs heavy. I suppose I could play around with that phrase, too, that I could easily go on like that—puff- ing my thoughts out like those robins in the bush, finding time for finding time for time.

From out of the past, win- dows laced with condensation. A past in which a girl stands looking out at a lawn that vanishes into thin air. From out of the past, the words of the ad: *Brylcreem, a little dab'll do ya*. Dabble in sound. *Yabba dabba do. Mairzy doats and dozy doats and little lamzy divvy. Itsy bitsy teenie weenie.* Teen age, with its white bucks and sock hops and jitterbugs reaching far into the future where they will be resurrected at a mere wisp of a tune. That boy with the surly smile. And that one, with his old maroon Dodge. They merge into one as they move in unison to *a white sport coat and a pink carnation.* Later, they will hum along—*Your baby doesn't want you any more* (dum dum dum dum dubba dubba dum), *it's over . . .* Orbison's voice breaking over their heads in a cascade of loss. A kid'll eat ivy too. Wouldn't you?

The silence is so pure. So uninterrupted. You can hear your father's paddle dipping in the water, can almost make out the faint flutter as water slides from it, back into water. *Shhh, shhh, shhh.* His paddle moves like clockwork, while yours is fickle. You want it to swing into accompaniment, but it seems to have an ornery mind of its own. Or maybe it's your muscles that don't seem in tune with your brain. The old mind/body conundrum, writ small. You are both there in the same canoe, in the same moment, but the moment belongs to no one. His canoe is steady while yours is capricious. It's a matter of experience, yes, but also of sensibility. His has always been steady, even when he was learning as a boy in Michigan. And yours will be capricious long into adulthood, and beyond, to where the only canoe you ride is memory, an erratic vessel at best. So go back to the silence, which can be broken at any moment. A bird will clatter its beak against branches. A frog will launch itself into the water, making a *thunk* that is part of the ongoing silence. The paddles speak for you as they dip and feather and dip, dip and feather and dip. A soft slap as water laps the shore—though do rivers have shores? Shouldn't they be banks? And don't banks have steeper sides, while this one has a gentle grade, almost imperceptible, like silence itself? Crickets buzz, and somewhere the oboe of a loon, though maybe it's only your idea of what a loon should sound like. Everything amplifies, even the silence, as you, *shhh*, paddle, *shhh*, into the magnified night.

She misses her father. Misses his way of opening out an argument and inviting discussion. She misses his red hair and his easy laugh and his faded blue eyes, but mostly she misses his way of having a conversation. Even when he got older and his opinions became carved in stone—in granite and marble, not the more compliant soapstone—he still loved a good, roundabout, circular discussion. She wonders if her own ideas aren't having a similar fossilization, but she hopes not. She thinks maybe she's limestone, a good middle-grade stone. Even that worries her, but you have to have some convictions, don't you?

Beckett lies on his back in the darkness and asks, "Who asks?" I am the one who is asking. I ask him why he is asking. I want to know if we are sharing the same space in a different time, or sharing the same time in a different space. I want to understand how his questions can become mine with one glance at the page. Can enter my head and swirl like a flock of quizzical birds. He can no longer ask and still he is asking.

Radiation. The closed box of it. The isolation. Lead rods clicking into place. Rotation of machine. Remote half-light. Held breath.

THE CIRCUS TRAIN

The sun hides for yet another day and this afternoon we will go to The Rose to see a movie. When we walk out, it will be dark. If this were June, the early-evening light would blind us. And now the dog in the yard across the street sounds so soulful. If this were night, he'd be coyote. So many if-this-weres in a lifetime of alternatives. It's a way of knowing what we might maybe once have known. Or at least suspected.

The sun hides and I ride the currents of summer. We are in Maine, watching the lobster boats making their rounds in the ocean below us. They interrupt the day with their greedy gulls and the stutter of their engines as they pause, then pull, then pause, then sputter toward the next brightly painted buoy, its odd comma suspending the sea. Look up, I think, as though I could will their attention. If this were winter, I would not be standing here. The water would be weary and cold. And if this were Vermont, summer would spell itself in bluebell and heal-all. If this were in the past, I'd be wading in Mulholland Creek where swarms of minnows haunt the shadows. And if this were in the future, I'd be sitting now, in this sunless room, knowing that when I went out I'd see water, water from every side, water that asks nothing of us as we take its limitless measure.

Of course she could go on, moment upon moment, measuring her days. Of course she could go on replaying scene after everyday scene. The words she spoke in anger. The ones she regrets. The ones she will not apologize for. But isn't she doing something else as well—asking her infernal questions? Isn't she adding it up, ticking it off, running it out? Isn't she looking for some way to make it make sense?

As though sense could save you! Honestly, nothing can save you, though you can save parts of yourself on the page. So there you are, 1:34 a.m., bludgeoning the keyboard with your late-night questions. Your memories piling up like so much driftwood. Or drifting out, as though the sea could steep them in the salt of memory. Enough. You're playing with words the way he did, and surely you want to do something else, to be the counterbalance.

THE CIRCUS TRAIN

And surely you realize how much ego is involved, using him as your model. But you've done that before, so who's to say you shouldn't emulate the best of them? Joyce and O'Brien and Beckett, those great jugglers of language. Those three very different lovers of life. Joyce with his words adding and adding, his sounds colliding, making their mesmerized meanings. O'Brien going in and under until her thoughts spill into someone else. Beckett subtracts, deducts, pulls away. "He speaks of himself as of another," he says into the dark, fashioning himself as a reticent character going on in perpetual present. In perpetual dark. And you, too, have created that infuriating "she" who stares back from the mirror. That maddening "you" who positions herself above the "I" that moves invisibly within, the pronoun we leave out when we speak to ourselves because—let's face it—we know who we're speaking to. No need for first person. Need to buy toilet paper. That sort of thing. Don't forget the mail. Admonish yourself. Or think in a different language, the way Beckett did, though *Company* kept company with his Dubliner English. Still, you can almost hear him talking to himself. *Écoute. Finis ton verre.* Drink up. Get on with it. Get on with lying on your back in

English while French crowds its way in the streets outside.

You never reached the point where you could move out of one syntax into another. In Rio, even Portuguese was softened to mush. A language of simple nouns: *beach, coffee, banana, song*. And if there were verbs, they were juvenile things: *play, like, eat, drink*. How hard could it be to say what you meant? Still, if you were not sure you were made for such unforgivable sun or those flamboyant flowers that sang their own praises, then there really were no words for your condition. No ready phrases.

Portuguese has one word that has no English equivalent. *Saudade.* How to define it? Nostalgia, yes, but nostalgia that carries with it a tinge of pleasure, the missing of something that calls up happy memories. *Saudade* for snow, for example, because the only snow is that of memory, and you will miss it acutely with a soft smile as you picture it spreading over the lawns, settling on fences until they carry their burden oh so lightly along their length, the celebration of cardinal or jay as they add their brief glint of color. Soft smile as you step out in boots to scoop up the past, letting it trickle over your face where you lick at its fake confection. Soft smile in perpetual summer twisting your heart where yes you miss snow you miss snow you miss snow.

Popsicles lining the freezer at Bosco's fruit stand. Lift the lid. One nickel for winter on your tongue.

Denmark has banned the use of trained wild animals in circuses. But what is "wild"? Oh, tigers—endangered and for decades deprived of the places they used to live. But elephants, who even in their native habitat will hold each other's tails and walk in tandem? The tractable ponies? I've seen ponies on Dartmoor, feral to the hilt as they fling their heads to note our passing. And dogs, for instance, can revert to their earlier selves, roaming in packs on the dusty streets of cities, or stalking their prey on vast savannahs. So the animals are banned, leaving entertainment to the trapeze artists who swing their

endangered selves over the failsafe nets,
the tumblers and tightrope walkers, the
unicyclists, the clowns. They'll ride in a
bus from town to town, recalling the days
when the train took them all—tigers in
their bright painted cages, monkeys and
elephants and prancing ponies—into its
constellation of cars.

The circus—the real thing.
Not the carnival, with its tin ear and its
come-hither deceptions. Its Ferris wheel
and the taste of Sno-Cones or funnel cakes.
I mean the circus, where acrobats show off
their years of practice, or clowns take on
personalities of their own. The carnival
doesn't last longer than that last throw of
the dart, that last toss of the ring. You walk
home with nothing but slum: the spider
rings and key chains and finger traps and
vampire teeth and fortune fish of the trade.
You walk past the charming tricksters—
Popeye and Smithy and Little John—who
stand there, calling you in, selling the
shabby dream to the highest bidder. They
dazzle you with the sound of their sugary
pitch. Because some things don't change all
that much over time, and the human desire
to win something for next to nothing is one

of them. The human desire to have some good fun being fooled.

Not the rodeo, either: calf roping, bulldogging, bronc riding, the whole dangerous show of it. But to watch a cowboy working his ranch . . . to watch his weathered face and the sheer determination of his will. The hard, lonely days where to lose a calf is to lose your farm, where to ride a horse is to know your land. And the land? Even against a backdrop of mountains, it stretches to where it disappears. A place so bleak and desolate that the meaning of beauty is called into question. A change in the horizon: ripple of ground, rocky outcropping, string of cattle, stand of cottonwoods, dilapidated shed poking its ribcage into the air—the land becomes an abstract painting, green against blue, yellow against blue, tan against gray, dark against light.

Tonight, a steadier, more constant rain. It resounds. Someone drumming fingers on the skylight, over and over. Not rhythm but algorithm. A drubbing. When it lets up, settles down, decreases, subsides, abates, the lack of sound will tug us into its tunnel. It will keep on making its no noise at all.

Ah, there it is, the "dummy pronoun"—what someone has dubbed the "ambient *it*." It is used so often we don't even notice. It rolls off our tongues before we can call it back. It has no referent, because none is needed. It has no trouble being understood on the other end—it is snowing, raining, sunny, hot, cold, in between. It is clear about its meanings. There's something to that. And that takes us to another term: the "existential *there*."

There were letters, back and forth, back and forth, crossing the country. Wings of thought, shards of her present. There was the anticipation, the sound of the mailman on the steps, the fingers tearing open the envelope, the reading. Then the response, licking the stamp, rushing to the post office. The waiting. Everything on hold while time crossed the country in its three-hour increments. There were letters, torn in half, so that her passion doubled in his desk. There were other things, but the letters say it all in their cursive version of what happened.

You—are you there?

There are days when you want to crush the little white pills and walk on out without them. There are days when the world asserts itself and you want to take it in. Its echo of imperfection.

"Ask me whether / what I have done is my life." Does your life really add up to the places you have been? And what you've done there? Stafford doesn't answer. He lets his mute river speak for him. Or almost.

You—if you're out there—I'd like to reach you. These events in our lives take up only seconds, minutes at best. You can measure their duration. Yet each one takes hours to set down on the page, to get it right, or

105

almost right. I'd like to tell you about desire and how it persists over time. Comes back full force. Takes the body by surprise. Maybe that knowledge could help you. Maybe not—you know how these things go: we don't learn other people's lessons.

Still, I know its dimensions and how they fade forward, so that earliest desire asserts itself with most intensity. Before the strawberry patch, there was no desire, and after, well, there it was. That doll, I wanted him so much I was afraid of the wanting. I was so sure he wouldn't be mine, and that my life would go forward with his absence at the center. Christmas was coming and I ransacked the house and he just was not there and I just didn't know how I would live without him, how I would put on my socks and drink all my milk and pick up my toys if he wasn't there. His name was Gregory Bruce, or so I heard it in the back of my head where I pretended I did not want him that much, not so much as to have already named him. And later, that bicycle, a whole year's worth of allowance until that fact alone seemed to be proof of my longing. That boy—surely we were too young, but still—with a grin that made me relax into the worn bench seat as though I had no cares in the world and, briefly, I didn't. Not my first husband so much as the moors he came from—the rust of heather and bracken and a sky so hollow you felt you might disappear. The small stone circles just off the footpath, and the path itself a vestige of a Roman road so straight it might be horizon. A longing for landscape so deep that it rose like the curlew whose song could be heard even though he had risen out of our sight. A call so urgent how could we do anything but calculate desire? And objects—the blown-glass bird or the lacquered box or the books upon books. Back to the man on the merry-go-round who will not look in my direction. Tell him about yearning. Tell him, from your distance, that someday we will live together in this house of bookshelves, so maybe he ought to begin to want right there, right then, when my horse cast its wild eye backwards.

Is this all there is? This quick, spent cartridge? Is this what it all adds up to?

JUDITH KITCHEN

She has *saudades* for her father, though she knows that is not the correct use of the word, not quite. It will have to do. She thinks of him when she encounters something she thinks he would have enjoyed. Or imagines something he might have said. She misses other people too, but not quite as much, not quite as often. She even misses in prospect, even though she has no prospects. Funny how the body resists knowing—really knowing—that it will shut itself down. Is that what we'd call the life force? She would probably resist that, because she's seen its awful undersides. The way denial leads to deception leads to hanging onto something so degraded that to call it life is senseless. Senselessness—that's what she wants when the body has stopped holding the mind, or when the mind insists itself beyond the body's wherewithal. Of that she is certain, just as she is certain that her father would agree with her; she can hear him now, though she had to beg the doctors not to call him up out of his husk.

"This should all be written in the pluperfect."

THE CIRCUS TRAIN

It had been raining and I had looked out my window to see a blooming of umbrellas, brightening the slick streets. Hundreds of umbrellas—yellow and red and green and, mostly, black—bobbing in and out and around each other, tentative at the gutter, then rushing across the street. Folding to ease their passage into doorways. It had been raining, and then, suddenly, it wasn't. But still the unseen people hurried on. I was in New York, standing at my window, and the rain had almost stopped. Planning my escape, planning a life I eventually never led. But I haven't stopped thinking how those umbrellas followed each other down the avenue.

It had been snowing—swarms of snow in the streetlight. Insects in the streetlight. And the streetlight itself hurling its feeble light into the storm. I had been watching snow fall into its orbit, then disappear. It had not seen me, ten years old, going on eleven. Going on to where I was heading. I had been thinking—thoughts so clear you could see them through the windowpane—and I had been both inside my room and out there swirling in the unruly night.

JUDITH KITCHEN

It had begun to snow again . . .

And then spring with its uncanny duplication: snowdrop, blood-root, wood anemone, crocus—and later that delicate, creeping blizzard along the runners.

Are you there? Can you hear what I have to tell you? Our lives are finite—and yet . . . Look at the way they preserve themselves. Think of all the bottom shelves harboring their photographs. Think of the disks filling with family. Think of all those old home movies, how they reel in your head. Think of the way I can still find my way to the house where I had my first babysitting job. Think of the way little Mikey, who died of leukemia, still has his name, still laughs when I come through the door. Here, I'll hand him over to you, the animated version: a boy of five with all his future before him.

She lies on her back, curled under the covers. Taking things into account. She thinks of Beckett, lying prone on his narrow bed, conversing with himself. The walk. The hand. Pizzicato. Committing to memory. Learning by heart.

Black cows in tall grass. A bit like boats in the marina, shifting with the current. I want nothing more than to think about the orderly comings and goings of cows.

There was one cow grazing on the mound at Newgrange. One cow, and five thousand years. Before the pyramids were built, long before Stonehenge, somewhere along the river Boyne, they (whoever they were) erected this monument, placed these stones with their megalithic drawings, the swirling patterns in which formlessness becomes form. They call it a Passage Tomb, and certainly we passed to its underground center where, in the dim light of flashlights, we could see shadows play on the walls, and the rounded stone basins where fragments of human bones had been found. Who knows why? There is no one left to tell. And there we were, stooping to walk into that cave, listening to explanations of how the roof box let in light precisely at dawn on each winter solstice. There we were, waiting for them (whoever they were) to replicate what it must have been like to wait in the darkness for the longest night of the year to end.

"To that perfect dark. That shadowless light. Simply to be gone." All his life, Beckett was drawn to that perfection. In that one word—*shadow-less*—shadows come alive. My uncle's fist, and on the wall suddenly a wolf opens his mouth. The squirrel's tail twitches, and the ground ripples black. My father reading, the lamp's strict perimeter. My mother at the clothesline, a skirmish of whipping sheets. The long companionable shadow stretching in front of me, then reeling itself in as noon approaches. My brother and I climb the maple tree and find our places among the leaves; the sun does not find us, yet we must be there somewhere in that kaleidoscope of motion on the ground. Simon jumping up and down on his slippery shadow, stamping it into the sidewalk beside the fountain. Two years old and he shouts at his shadow, laughs, and there he is—now—leaping through time after his intangible twin. I imagine it so fully—Ian streaking down the field, the ball a shadow of a ball as it flies over the grass toward him. Matthew's flickering profile, on then off. I remember William swinging on a vine at Parque Lage, swooping down to meet his double on the jungle floor. Stan reaches for the brass ring and the carbon copy of his arm appears beneath him, caught where sunlight snags the far edge of the merry-go-round. Our plane descending until—there—its growing outline rises up to meet it. Thump. We're here. We are not gone, not even tangentially. We simply carry this quiver of shadows with us.

"Till finally you hear how words are coming to an end. With every inane word a little nearer to the last. And how the fable too. The fable of one fabling with you in the dark." She hears Beckett talking himself out of the company he has invented. She has her own fables—ones that extend beyond the dailiness that seems, suddenly, so substantial. She has fables that involve decisions she has been asked to make, and the ones that seem to have been made for her. In another time, those would have been called fate.

JUDITH KITCHEN

Memory rides its own horse, and you cannot stop it. It makes a wide, white wake in which seasons merge. Sometimes memory pools like standing water in a field, still and exact, reflecting an empty sky. You sit in the saddle and watch what you meant to do vanish behind you.

Simon is holding a chicken. Feathers the color of his hair. I was not there. I have only the memory of the photograph. Second-hand, once-removed. Split second reduced to replica.

The boys don't like parades, they tell her. They'd rather explore the back yard. Kick a ball. Unearth their grandfather's old toys in the attic. So she sits alone on her old front stoop, watching the majorettes in crisp blue and white, the high school band, half in step, fire trucks with their flashing lights, veterans shuffling. She knows what will come. The whole shebang will round the corner and disperse at the cemetery gate. The Gettysburg Address. In Flanders Fields. Taps. How the weakening sound of rifles will ricochet along the line of hills.

THE CIRCUS TRAIN

Messi dances, turns, just one touch on the ball, and it lifts to the top of the net. Pure instinct, you might say. Or sure knowledge. How many days did he make this one move, practicing for what we now term precision? How many times did he fail before he learned to make art?

Fail better. Fail best. Fail safe. Fail to fail. Weather the storm. Stormy weather—and now we are back in the Bronx, eight of us packed into a tiny bar, listening as the singer lowers her low voice, turns it husky with desire. The two of you look at each other through the threat of covered mirrors. *Keeps rainin' all the ti-ime,* the long *i* held and held until the raindrops are suspended in air, where they still reside, mummified in memorial air.

What can I call this associative process? Emulsion of intersected lives? Fusion of tenses? Loves found, loves lost, all blended in a fleeting swirl of molecules. What can I say for the assonance that leads to this torrent of words? This is not erasure, but profusion. Infectious. It has little to do with what was said to whom, but what was taken in. What color would you call it? Black—nuance upon nuance—one tint on top of another on top of another on top of . . . until the black of the crow on the telephone wire, so dark he seems like a cutout against the sky, and yet we know the colors are there—look how they shimmer on his wings as he preens and puffs his feathers. Or white, the absence of choice, and still it persists in snow, in primrose, eggshell and waterfall, in the harsh, unresponsive page.

It's a matter of balance. You inch yourself forward without looking down. You hold the pole in front of you, letting it offset the body's pull. You waver, then steady. Below you, there is no net.

Unsteady on your pins, your father would have said, though he was never unsteady on his. Laugh at yourself as you bump into chairs, veer toward the doorframe. This is not a body you can count on. You remember what it was like when your body took root in the ground. You belonged to the earth even as you ran across it, even as you skimmed its creekbeds and stomped in its puddles. "The roots of language are

irrational and of a magical nature," said
Borges, and you realize that the body, too,
is rooted in grammar. Your muscles learned
the derivation of movement, and now the
dictionary is letting them down. So start
again at the toes. The ones your infant self
could put in its mouth. The ones that eventually knew the torture of hot asphalt and
the ache of high-heeled shoes. Start there
and learn how to walk.

Step onto the ferry. Soon it
will leave the slip and head across the Sound.
It will churn its way through the water and,
if the day is nice, you can stand on the deck
watching the wake recede. If Simon is young,
you will watch with him for the gulls he calls
"awk-awks" and you will follow him around
and around as he discovers the world. If he
is older, he will be more sedate, choosing
something to drink and talking to you about
school. He will flick his hair out of his eyes.
If he is older still, you will need to imagine
the young man you may never see. He will
find a seat somewhere in the bow and he'll
peer out intently, searching for the place he
remembers you waiting when he came across
as a child. Why not let him grow into middle age, and beyond? Why not have the sense

of completion any good book could give you?
Any good book . . . and you have to question
just what you are doing. This could be called
a pre-posthumous memoir. Come to think
of it, aren't they all? But in reclaiming your
life, you realize how ordinary it must have
been, that you should have to make drama
out of something as mundane as sitting in
a strawberry patch. If there had been major
consequence, maybe you would not now
resort to those commonplace roots. The ones
that branch out beneath the soil, decidu-
ous. Honestly. No, that doesn't capture your
voice. Honestly! That's better. That's the real
power of the exclamation point—the way,
way back then, Simon could point to the
gulls and even his finger would highlight his
tone.

      Through the skylight, a hint
of moon. In ambient light, the eyes adjust,
make out the shapes of alarm clock, lamp-
shade, chair. Somewhere out there, a raccoon's
eyes blaze. An owl drops. Overhead, one lone
plane, faint rumble in the 3:00 a.m. sky. Where
is it going at this late, early hour? Above the
cloud cover, a droning, fainter, then gone. And
afterwards a silence that lasts and lasts and fills
up the dark with its absence of sound.

THE CIRCUS TRAIN

$\mathbf{Y}$ou out there—I hope you're there, because I need you. I need someone to carry this project forward, to write back into a past that is beginning here. And now. You won't be using decoder rings or *Our Miss Brooks* on the radio. No, you'll start with smart phones and Kindles, Darth Vader movies, sneakers with lights in their heels. Digitized, somethingized—whatever will be the next science fiction in the making. Whoever you are, I hope you are watching the world go past. Your world, and your inner world within it. Look up. Take out your Bluetooth and listen. The water makes a sound as the ferry moves through it. Rips open. Overhead the mayhem of gulls is persistent. Everything persists, even as everything changes. So keep a close watch. I'll want an accounting. I'll want to know whether memory itself can be eroded if there's no one to decode its messages, no one to sort out its meanings and give it its newly coined nouns.

$\mathbf{E}$verything changes and everything stays the same. I know that's not a new insight, but to feel it in my bones—that's new for me. To see my grandsons at Thanksgiving and realize that they will carry

on some of these same traditions. These same
feelings. This same pleasure at seeing their
own grandchildren. That they will look out
the window and see the year winding down,
and they may remember this one day when
we cooked a dish of butternut squash. Maybe
the smell of squash will call up this day, and
it will be the same day and I will be there. I
will be caught in the arc of my hand stirring
and I will hover over the stove, turning to
smile at the three men I do not know. And
yet know. I hope in their remembering they
will find room for it all—the ferry, the beach,
the hula-hoops on the back deck. The fawns
flinging themselves at the fence. And they
will wonder what their children will remember of them as they stand by the window, not-
ing the mysterious way the same leaves seem
to have returned each year, and those leaves
are now dropping to the ground as though to
release their turbulent shade.

"Blind guess" the doctor
called it, but I am living in today's bright
sun as though it were the first day.

Strange how suddenly a word
you've lost will reappear, as though dropped

120

in the ear by accident. Then there it is—the lake, smooth as glass, almost opaque. There it is, waiting for your body to inch its way in, or embrace the torture and dive. The water is cold. It takes getting used to. You hop up and down and you look to the shore to call "watch me" but no one really wants to watch because they are adults and you are the child so you cup and punch the water, a slap and a splash that will carry the sound down through decades until your body feels permanently cold.

P̲unch Bowl Lake!

J̲ust so, one word. Sound asserting dominion. The images recur— they return and return. They well up when they are most needed. We use them as touchstone, benchmark, hallmark, yard-stick—those compound words of accretion. They tell us how to "read" our lives. Or, at the very least, to measure it. To return to the strawberry patch is to become aware of self as distinct from others. Though I am told my first sentence was "My do it!"—imply-ing a sense of independence long before I see myself sifting the dirt into affable silence. To go back to the merry-go-round might

JUDITH KITCHEN

imply adults reverting to childhood, but I like to think of it more as the marvel of being suspended between past and future. To conjure the circus train . . . It must have meant something as it moved across my horizon and vanished into the haze. It must have meant something, because it keeps on trailing its scarf of smoke

Coda

Okay, the mind plays its own tricks. So go
for what is certain. As in *honest.* Let the rest
of your life be free from fraud. Even the petty
pretenses that cover your real feelings and
make the day go round. If you're bitter, be
bitter, I say. If you're blunt, be blunt. I remember the day she read the most honest sentence
she had ever seen. Or that's how it feels to her
now. She must have been in seventh grade,
filled with all she did not know. Her hair in a
ponytail and her plaid skirt falling just below
her knees. The boys had taunted her all day,
laughing because she liked to read. Laughing
their way under her skin.

> *In the fall the war was always there,*
> *but we did not go to it any more.*
> —Ernest Hemingway, *Men Without Women*

If she could write a sentence like that, she
could penetrate the past. Go straight for the
heart of it.

The lodge in New Hampshire where we stayed
in a little white cottage and ate in the Inn's
dining room with windows looking out over

an expanse of lawn to the White Mountains.
We can both agree that was real, can't we?
The morning mist. Hiccup of a breeze. The
mountains tame. Nothing like the jagged,
dark edges of Macgillycuddy's Reeks behind
the cottage we rented outside Killarney. The
one where we both stepped back in time.

Let's play it again for the sake of discovery.
What is behind memory? Beside it? Below?

In the fall . . . and suddenly there you are,
ironing a mottled red maple leaf between
squares of waxed paper, tipping it into your
book where it may or may not surface in
some future year. You love the season—the
pumpkins, the pitter of leaves dropping
from trees, skittering along the sidewalk.
The deep-set days. Everything round and
perfect as the word *October.*

The war . . . you have never seen war,
but you have imagined it. Felt its restless anxiety as a kind of background
noise. You were born during a war—
the one that meant rationing books and
no rubber for tires and soldiers coming

home. Then Korea, Cold War, Vietnam. And far away—Iran-Iraq—the way war has of coming back bigger, if not better. You have seen its aftermath: rubble kept intact as reminder. And then, too, the Berlin Wall, now also rubble. The man in Devon who came to the table to thank the Americans for what they had done. What had they done? They had gone over, come over, lived through, rescued, and released, that's what. They went to the war.

Was always there . . . so that the long, slow wash of time was held in abeyance, while in the streets people walked, made small talk, and nothing appeared out of the ordinary except for the ordinary. Odd, how the body accommodates, gets used to, adjusts, adapts. How "always" becomes a constant.

But we did not . . . no, never. We did, do, not. We hide behind the negative, as though the word "not" was all that stood between us and action. If not war, then how else have we failed to act? We did not dance. How trivial. Still, that's the way I would complete the sentence, letting all its desire drain out on the sand. We did not dance that night away, and now it's too late. The body no longer imagines the waltz.

Go to it any more . . . though there's no "it" to go to. At least not one with an "any more" to round it out, prop it up, push it along. Any more. In time. In amount. In addition. The phrase presupposes a future, but the future, now, seems so finite. So terribly finished.

It was a cold fall and the wind came down from the mountains.

Here's what Hemingway managed to convey: a tone so simply honest. No adjectives to mar its stark, straight-forward sense of being on the cusp. On the edge of a mountain. The brink.

Though substitute "sea" for "war" and you hear in your head the missing tides, but there's nothing to take you into reverie. The memory of self standing on a beach, maybe, looking out to the horizon, looking west. So many seas. Just say Firth of Forth and the day goes cold and moody. Say Copacabana

and waves rise, convulsive, under a molten
sky. Damariscotta: the green Atlantic surges
and swells. The noun will do to muster lobster boats or the little lighthouse at the end
of the spit. Here, in our tiny Northwest
town, the sea is gray, glossed with the sheen
of undercover sun. In Hemingway—the
Mediterranean writ large as, far below, it
glitters a forthright blue.

*We came down around curves, through deep dust,
the dust powdering the olive trees.*

We came down around curves and we—you and
I—are there, simply rounding the bend to
where the scene unfolds. Though we—you and
I—have never been to Italy. Or not together.
Our memories chase each other through the
haze of orchards. The mottled leaves. The
wine, the canopy of shade. The road uncoil-
ing as it dips down to the sea. But we don't go
there. We go to places we share, places where
the air is strident. Lupine. Or dogwood. And
the river noisy in its rush to go somewhere.

That lodge—that's where we stayed an extra
day to cook a meal for the bicyclists. The

owner's girlfriend left him on the eve of a big commitment: she'd arranged for thirty cyclists to eat and stay overnight. What could he do? So we volunteered. Turkeys to dress. Lasagna to make. Huge stainless steel bowls, roasters, and pans. Wine to buy. Carrots to peel. Who ever cooked for thirty, who knew proportions, who knew the waiting baskets of bread? We worked all day and then left before the cyclists arrived. So who knows how it all turned out? Its dimensions?

And the bicyclists, who were they? A bunch of ten-speeds locked together at the trailhead. A long line of reflective vests slowing traffic on their way uphill, slowing the day to a monotonous round of pedal, pedal, push, push, next and next and next. A collective *whoosh* down toward the streambed. A hungry hoard at the gate. Bought. And paid for.

Not one face to recognize. Not one to remember. Not an adjective among them. Only the fact of their upcoming presence. Though we can conjure the fresh white napkins. The silverware laid out in rows. The owner in his T-shirt, lost in his excess of worry, his whirlwind breakup. So what is memory but the sum of syllables? Clouds piling up in the sky and the mountains suddenly menacing. Our car pulling out of the drive, leaving him there to muddle his way through the slicing and serving and smiling while, all the while, his heart was not there, not there at all. While, all the while, the argument ticked through his head, and each time he heard it, he knew he was right, so why did he miss the details? Her hard-hearted laughter. Her bare arm brushing his shoulder. Her wild mouth a billow of smoke. Her mean, tormenting jokes. Her painted toenails. Her loud, ringing disrespect.

See how difficult it is! Even the doctor asks for adjectives, asks you to describe the cough. Is it dry? Or raspy? The adjective reigns. But the cough itself—you lie in bed at night listening to the faint after-purr of air making its low rumble in your left lung. You cough again, your body tugging at its seams. You try to lie still, but the body rebels. You hold the cough drop in your mouth, carefully, carefully, so you won't suck it in, choking on what might help you. You lie in the dark and you worry away at description—as though anyone wants to know the dimensions of your cough, the scope of it. Though

the stethoscope was cold on your skin, and
he heard it, yes, that place where your wings
would be if you had wings, the crepe paper
rustle that provides confirmation.

Why, she asks, does the exact sequence matter so much to her, the exact words—said
where, and when? When he tells the story,
it does not feel like the life she has lived.
False note, when what she wants is the tun-
ing fork of what was.

The cough filled the car. Riddled. Wracked.
Though riddled implies holes punched
through, and wracked feels more like
twisted iron. But this was both at once—
raddled, wricked—and her fever added to
the commotion. The bridge stretched its
lyre over the water. Her lungs that taut,
that musical.

In the spring, the cough was still there, but
we didn't hear it any more. It had become a
part of us. Not something we might mention as in *remember that cough?* but something
ubiquitous, a given, a state of being, if you
will. In the spring, we were in a state of

uncertainty again, and the trees came alive without us.

What she wanted was the solidity of the noun. What Stevens called *The the*. Though Stevens was not where she went for solace. She thought of him as a poet of adjectives, and when she went back to the poems, she saw there were not as many as she had remembered. But still, his nouns were less than solid. It was Frost she turned to. His ability to say it plain so she knew where she was and where she was coming from. *The tribute of the current to its source*—and she could see the stream interrupt itself, ripple backwards at each stone's insistence, water rising white to the surface, swirling backflip—a cough—before it settles into the wider expanse that drifts past at its own pace. Swift enough to make its muffled gurgle, slow enough to look, for a moment, as though everything were steady state. Stream. One word. No need for anything else.

The "I" has mostly disappeared. Resurrected in memory as someone who used that pronoun. Who walked into a room with the I intact—sensibility, and a sense of ownership. More and more, the I lives in a past that is non-negotiable. It was. It is. And to think that it will evaporate—just like that—like water struck by sun, and no one can retrieve it. Maybe the shared memory . . . But that is suspect, always vanishing into another point of view. The I would like to retain perspective. The I would like to know *why* it wasn't going to the war any more. Why those words called out to a girl with a plaid skirt, a future ahead of her that she fully intended to go to.

Near Knaresborough in North Yorkshire a small stream flows downhill, drops over a rocky overhang into the River Nidd, turning anything in its path to stone. It was near this petrifying well that Mother Shipton—considered a witch—made her famous prophecies. Much of what she foretold came true. Could that be called the opposite of memory? We stood there, looking up to where objects had been tied under the lip of the rock: teddy bears, baby shoes, teakettles, cricket bats—people's lives, memorized in stone. We stood there, watching water work to contradict itself. Petrify: transitive verb. To solidify, yes, but also to terrify.

THE CIRCUS TRAIN

What verb would you choose for the way those redwing blackbirds landed on the cattails? They came in for a landing, for sure, but was it hard or soft? Swift or leisurely? Did they bank and circle, or simply head like an arrow for their target? All I know is that it is possible to feel the arc of their flight, and hear their *ck-ck-wa-heeeeee* filling the distance. They seem always to be plundering the pond, or perched at the spiky tip, chipping away at the day.

There were days when the soccer field seemed to glow in slant October light, and boys flew across it, the checkered ball incidental to their youth and energy. Two of the boys were my sons and their long legs surprised me. In the shadows of early evening, I was a red car, a ride home. I hold them there, knowing in hindsight some of what has become of their lives. But none of us knew more than that moment of eloquence when the ball spilled before them like water.

See? I remember bicyclists I did not see. I remember my thoughts of them as I stuffed the turkeys, patted on butter, tucked the aluminum wrap. But I did not see them swoop through the gate and pull up to the porch, yanking off helmets, dusty and tired, soft laughter in the front of the pack, a groan behind. In my mind, they threw down their bikes and spilled onto the grass, and the owner came out to greet them. There was the smell of woodfire, of cauliflower and cucumber and, softly, the cinnamon of apple pies we'd also left behind. And where were we? Somewhere long gone, somewhere on the road to home, past Vermont, maybe almost to the Adirondacks. They spilled out on the lawns as solid and certain as if we were there. The girlfriend? They were in her mind, too—the final indignation of a final fling with someone who simply took what she had to offer without offering much in return. She was well rid of him. And the bike club—it could eat store-bought frozen food for all she cared.

Sometimes it's something so small you wonder why you've kept it at all. A window seat. Curtains lifting in the breeze, then falling back, lifting, falling back, lifting, falling back like a butterfly wing, all afternoon, all afternoon. A barn with its great high ceiling and sunlit streaks of dust swarming in the

rafters. So small, and yet there they are, adding one day to the next to the next on the
way to this one.

Sometimes the scene is vivid—the huge locomotive churning into the station, hissing as
it grinds to a stop. The huge wheels dwarf-
ing everyone. And your grandmother stepping
down with her leather suitcase. Her solid black
shoes. Her braid. Sometimes hazy, as the curtain
lifts and falls back somewhere—where?—some
time when you were small and mesmerized.

Middle of April, middle of the day. The eye-
lids grow heavy. Not a nighttime fatigue,
but a shutting down. The fever crawls up the
spine, eases its way into the ear, the throat.
The thermometer ticks off its degrees. The
body flares. The eye closes, lets in the time
the girl stepped down from the bus, climbed
the wide steps and entered the cool interior
of the library where, because she knew the
girl would be there, Miss McCabe had put
aside a stack of books. She'd broken the rules
for this girl, giving her books from the Adult
section—Hemingway first, then Fitzgerald,
Faulkner last. Not a woman among them,
though sometimes she felt guilt when she

passed by Cather on the shelves. Passed by the girl's place in the world in favor of places Miss McCabe had never seen: France, New York—she'd never even been to New York—the furtive heart of Mississippi. Let the girl enter the stream, feel the words flow around her ankles, swirl, and move on, taking her with them. Let the girl have a life she could call her own, not this musty cave in a middle-sized city where the streets were all called First, Second, or Third, or, for variety, the name of the rivers—Tioga, Chemung.

You have a past of your own, and I do not believe you when you say "this is what was"—there are too many places where our stories do not settle their differences. Behind the pickets, a deer in camouflage. Flick of tail. Of ear. Lifting of hind leg. Strobe effect. The tail again, here, then there, as though several small birds were flitting in the branches. When she appears—the whole of her—casually strolling onto our lawn, she looks up and then ignores us. She owns the place. There's no other interpretation.

Somewhere poppies burst into flame. The sheer, fierce heat of them. Stone walls make their way over the moors. Wind fingers the back of the neck; a man walks the horizon; a curlew calls. The girl does not know what a curlew sounds like, but still the call rises into clear air. The story unfolds, red as the poppies, red as the earth, red because its primary status insists on an adjective. If she could do without it, she would.

1963. Edinburgh, Scotland. A young woman hurries down Thistle Street to Number 11—Chambers Publishing Company—where she will take an antiquated elevator to the fourth floor. There Miss Agnes Macdonald, eighty years old, will open the door to her knock and take from her the edited version of the letter S. All week the young woman has pored over dictionary entries, weeding out the words she will omit, weeding out the most obscure definitions of the words she is keeping, working and working to replace single-word definitions with phrases, then using the selected words in sentences. All week, she has found herself sitting at the top of double-decker buses, crisscrossing the city, listening to how teenagers talk. Now she will hand over the typewritten pages she has produced. It is spring outside and the cobblestones give back the sunlight. Flowers are growing in the

JUDITH KITCHEN

Princes Street Gardens. It is still winter in
Miss Macdonald's attic office, and she may or
may not offer a cup of tea. She may or may not
reveal the seven layers of clothing she wears to
keep warm. Miss Macdonald will thank the
young woman, then take out a pair of scissors
and carefully cut out the pages for T, hand
them to her for the next few weeks' work. She
may or may not show her her spidery scrawl
on the pages for R, which she has reserved
for herself. But something will happen there,
as the dictionary is bandied between them,
the words that together they've chosen to preserve performing their slow pantomime. All
winter, the young woman has lived on words,
cashing her meager check, then returning to
the cold-water flat she shares with her husband with crumpets from the local bakery.
All winter, the dictionary has ebbed and
flowed, and soon the job will be over. U-V-W-
X-Y-Z. She hopes they will see her through
to summer. Fifty years later, the woman will
open the faded orange and green cover and
be surprised at the simplicity of the definition: *n.* the warmest season of the year—in
cooler northern regions May or June to July or
August—Also *adj.*—*v.i.* to pass the summer.
It will be spring, summer still a premonition.
It will be spring and she will be wary of memory, its uncanny accuracy.

THE CIRCUS TRAIN

On the television, an April blizzard. As in whiteout. Route 80 across Wyoming closed. When she was there, it had been the middle of May, long enough ago to call it her past. Gates barred the road at every exit out of Laramie. Snow sweeping into town—a heavy, wet invasion. And then over! Sun wiping the city clean again, so they could drive on west, then south on the loneliest dirt road they'd ever seen. No car for hours in either direction, though horse trailers were parked by trails that led off over square miles of ranch land. Where were the invisible men who rode under that intemperate sky?

Unnecessary memory. Useless collection in the junk drawer of your mind: the telephone number of your eighth grade friend, the price of shoes in 1960, your great-grandfather's middle name, names of babies you've never met, names of streets and towns and counties. Names of old lovers. Names for love.

Unbidden memory. Refrain. Reprise. Over and over—aria da capo—he turns his back, leaving her forsaken, though she sat so still she could hardly breathe. She sat so still that even in the present those scenes have no verb.

Obsolete: steam engine, record player, roller skate key, running boards, clotheslines, elevator man, house calls, Sunday hats, Selectric typewriter—Q-W-E-R-T-Y-U-I-O-P—the little silver ball twirling and twirling. Spiral down into your past and you only go deeper into its fog. The dog at the end of the block. The hold-out oaks, the crisp hands of their leaves clinging to the branch long past Christmas. Everything moves in consonance with your deepest dreams. The past sways in a long, slow dance. Memory makes of our lives what they were, what they weren't.

Sometimes we need to learn to remember. My grandfather drove a horse and buggy, coming to the automobile late in his life. He used to shout "whoa" before he would step on the brakes. The times table, fixed so early in the mind, begins to unravel. I need to think twice about 8 x 7, 12 x 11. The litany of general obligations: Tuesday exercise, Thursday garbage, first Wednesday meeting, unless it

THE CIRCUS TRAIN

falls on the 1ˢᵗ, then second Wednesday.
Still, I hold to the discrete moments that
matter—the where, when, why of them.
The what—now that's a different story.
"What" contains consequence. And consequence contains corollary. And corollary
contains upshot. Outcome.

We went to soccer games in the old stadium
where trains screamed past three or four
times a game—freight trains trailing their
yellows and deep reds across our line of sight,
or passenger trains with their bright strip of
silver light. The skyline grew dark and lights
winked on in office buildings across the river.
On the field, the players moved up and down,
back and forth under the floodlights, and
we watched their elaborate weavings with
fixed attention. Attend. Intransitive verb. Pay
attention to what the heart calls up: those
trains streaking toward commemoration.

Does remember count as a verb? Its action
the making of action.

And who will be left to remember these days
of uncertainty? The sheer difficulties, the

small satisfactions. The ordinary life going on being ordinary. Yet ordinary is what we strive for in our sense of going on, going forward, going where we simply have to go. Who will be left to contain the past—our particular past, the one we have shared— when we can no longer state it? So I state it now. You were there with me.

It was a cold spring and the rain would not stop falling. The road dropped down to the strait, and the sea was dull and still. Foghorns broke into the morning. Crows huddled in bunches along the telephone wire, and the wind carried their sounds down to where the wet earth waited. Other birds came frequently to the feeder, but we didn't hear them. We sat by the window looking out at the doe flickering in the garden.

Coda: is it afterthought or addendum? The sea with its measureless verbs.

In Three Parts

But leaving is only conditional. The person you are,
is anathema to the person you would like to be.
—Edna O'Brien, *Mother Ireland*

My hair has come back darker, thinner,
less like the person I thought I was. More
a shadow of myself. I will have get used
to seeing this person with the moon face,
the wisps of hair that grow unruly overnight, need water to tame them. I stand
in the doorway, watching the rain. A
pounding rain. Eastern. It reminds me of
childhood—gutters swelling, our T-shirts
soaked and streaming, our voices shouting
hoooo-eeeee in the summer storm. I think of
myself as still ten, still that boundless din
of a girl.

The tree dropped its circle of black on
the lawn—green-black—the color of
the bottom of a pond. There were two of
them—a he and a she—and they stood

143

in its cool deliberation. Now everything
mattered, and they didn't know what to
do about that. Thoughts flew off. Blue,
like the wingtip of a jay. He remembered
the day she reached her hand across the
table. She remembered the day he tum-
bled into her attic room as though they
were doomed. And they were, as we all
are, destiny being what it is—an unreli-
able narrator at best. Under the tree, they
cast themselves as lovers peering out into
sunlight. Bright time asked nothing of
them but to take it in, like laundry fresh
from the windblown line, or the smell of
newmown hay—images from a past they
never shared: milk brought in glass bot-
tles to the doorstep, mail delivered twice
each day.

One, two, three, and there, on three, the hand
flips out, flat, covering the rock, vulnerable
to scissors. One, two, three and there it is, the
stuff of your trade. Paper white as the snow
that drifts at the edge of memory, spreading
across the field to where blue shadows pool
in the footprints. White as snowdrops filling
the lawn for an instant, then gone under an
onslaught of rain. Blank. Both a beckoning
and an erasure. Black words, where are you?

THE CIRCUS TRAIN

What do you mean to fill as you find your
own fulfillment?

The word was indelible, though it came
over the phone and was gone in an instant.
Invisible. But still audible, ringing in the
ears. Metastasis. So the hour of the beginning
of the rest of my life was fixed: 2:30 p.m., on
a bright May afternoon. Fixed in the QFC
parking lot, of all places, groceries being
loaded into trunks, the stuff of life—oranges
and broccoli and yogurt and Tide—rising up
as if they could ward off the word's odd final-
ity. Then the drive home under the flickering shade of cedars and pines, putting away
the milk and the coleslaw, wondering who
am I beyond this time-bomb ticking?

Already the mind deflects the word, with its
one clear definition. Already the mind plays
its tricks. Down to brass tacks. Down to the
wire. Down to the bone. Downbeat, down-
cast, downfallen, downhearted, down under.
Or almost.

Made in the shade, we say, as though sun
would expose us for what we are: mortal, and

therefore vulnerable, and therefore certainly not made in the shade. Not at all. Nope. Nix. As a verb. To cancel, revoke, rescind. Kaput. As in leave, leaving, left.

Left alone, who would I like to be? I try on the possibilities, the way I try on a new blouse, or the way I imagine the alternative lives I might have led—the ones that offered themselves to me before I made choices that sent them reeling into a receding past. A past that can rise any time to taunt me with what I gave up, giving myself over to what I have become.

In the other life, the one half-lived, she sees what she never saw before: the dark bar's deep interior where, every Saturday night, her son played guitar with his band. Nearly three decades later, there he is—his familiar form on a Facebook video—the dynamic past clamoring for attention. Look at the way he bends his body into the music, the way he turns his back on everyone. He's lucky, she thinks, lucky to have known what he didn't want. He flicks his long hair out of his eyes and turns in her direction: a slim young man whose vanished notes still ripple outward, gloriously sullen and cynical.

That stream in Vermont, the way it was really mere trickle beside the road, more a tumble of rocks, homage to origin. Moss-covered stones. Shadows flickering like fish in the deeper pools. Walk into the woods. Hold yourself still in a past you've almost forgotten. Listen . . . the sound of time moving forward, soft swish of silken time, punctured only by birdcall, and your own breath making its steady racket: in, then out, in, then out, accordion of air.

Suppose I did not board that ship all those years ago. Quit everything, stayed in New York. I see myself turning in at a wide doorway, climbing the steps to an office spread with manuscripts. I see myself reading and reading, sifting and sorting, then back down the stairs to dinner at a sidewalk café under an umbrella's synthetic shade. Everything but the man—really the boy—I turned from as I walked up the gangplank. I see myself with the ghost of a past, a man I might catch sight of on the street, a man

I knew, even then, could give me no future. I look up, that glint of expectation. Not him. But still, one day it might be—it's not against all odds. What will we say to each other? After the "is that you? Is that really you? What a coincidence!" After that, what would we say? I see myself, silly with the dream now so diminished. But still, there would have been the city—the white sky pulling the eye upwards. The pages and pages of sky.

Back-fire of memory. Controlled burn.

Who will be left to remember the Mynah bird pacing his cage at the Edinburgh Zoo? "Where's Charlie? Where's the pretty boy?" over and over, in his little old-man's voice. His head cocked so his eye was on a plane with yours. Looked you straight in the eye as he called and called for his oddly lost self.

If you had stayed in New York, she tells herself, you would have lived in a tiny second-floor apartment, windows looking out on one stumpy tree, on sidewalk and shops that displayed their awnings by day and metal grids over their doorways at night. A hint of green somewhere far away. The tips of trees. And grass? You would have longed for grass and the way it rose up to meet your toes. You would have become one of those quick-footed anonymous people who lose themselves in the chaos of the day. Who stop at the corner to buy a clear plastic container of salad. Who sit at night reading and reading, the light of the window marking their solitude, their all-too-single lives. If you had stayed in New York, face it, you would have looked him up and waited outside his building and pretended you just happened to be there and watched him pretend to believe you and there you would be, caught in a chaos of your own making as he extricates himself, turns, walks out of your life for a second time.

In the perpetual shade of skyscrapers, the grass is pale, and impatient. It never really quite sees the sun. She walks by this spot every so often and notes its grays and greens. Its little liver spots of brown. Then, she sees him. She is so sure. But when his profile turns to meet her eyes, it's someone else, someone younger than he would be by now.

There are words for it all, but they belong to characters in the books and the books already belong to the past. To the swift, sharp seclusion of the past, and memory that hones itself on its whetstone.

THE CIRCUS TRAIN

II.

The grass was soaking, and now in the sunshine
shadows moved and pranced over it like the hooves of
phantom horses. Shadows neither green nor black
but sage.
—Edna O'Brien, *House of Splendid Isolation*

She has seen that color in the tropical forest,
where sunlight is filtered to a hint of green.
Where shadows stand still. It's the sunlight
that stutters—on, then off, then on, tracing
the trunks. What if the family had stayed in
Brazil, the boys suddenly easy in Portuguese,
enough to tease her that she'd never lost her
accent? She'd have the grammar, but not the
inflection. If you could hear your own bad
accent, you'd change it, wouldn't you? Their
sense of winter would fade, and white would
mean beaches bleaching in the sun, the
whitewash of waves breaking, and breaking.
Maria sem vergonha (Mary without shame)
spilling its loose, almost-lascivious blossoms
at the edge of the jungle. Churches with
their wide stone steps. Cast-iron, obstinate
sun. The lens on her camera would open to
this new land and the self she thought she

was would disappear. The slate wiped clean. How do you retain a self unless in words? She looks up now, knowing that this life would have left her bereft. Her sons as she knows them would have been swallowed in the spume of otherness. The page of dislocation.

Even England, with its coverlet of fog, would have shaken her identity. Those bells—their radiant surprise. Those moors, their scrupulous histories. Who would she be in her size 27 shoes, her scarf wound tight against the wind? Who would she sound like when she talked to herself? That life scrolls out along the canal and she cannot find herself crossing the bridge, waving from the other side. She cannot find herself in her splendid isolation.

A dapple of sidewalk, while we rode our bicycles in and out of the durable summer sun. The tree was an elm. An elm from before the days when elms had all but disappeared. Its leaves sent their shade in fluted ovals—fluid—scuttling over the lawn. We rode back and forth, testing the way the pupils could dilate in the darkened interior realm, then close again under an onslaught of light.

THE CIRCUS TRAIN

The tree was an elm, and it was doomed,
but no one knew. It was merely shade, and
its color was caught between then and now.

What is your mood as you face each day with
a shadow of doubt? The unreconstructed word
trailing its tiny *if* behind your every move?
Who would you be without the nagging
weight on your shoulders? Would you laugh
without shame? Or would you simply not
realize how light your load was, how bright?

Downpour of words littering the tongue,
forgotten words like icebox, calliope, canopy, and somewhere summer stammering.
Torrent of words battering the page, bar-
tering, bantering, dropping their two-tone
shades into the simmering grass. Step back.
Listen to the crickets whipping dusk to a
frenzy while shadows start to fray. There was
a he and an I. No story starts without them.
So how will it be when the I drops away?
Black circle dotting the i of the eye of the
bird facing down the dark.

The answer to every question begins with *if*
and ends with *if.* The subjunctive. The what

is not happening, but might. The what is almost wanted. The condition of *as if* or *if not for* that knocks on the door and then lets itself in. The sun rises high in the sky, day after day after day, and still the answer is framed in the unknown.

And where is Itaipu, little canary, locked in his wooden cage? Thirty years lost, he's still singing, still caught in sunlight filtered through turquoise shutters. Still he opens his beak, his high notes filling the forest of air—the sea of air—for an instant before he settles back, glum, as though he were not what he meant himself to be, not at all.

Right now—this minute—she is whining. You might call it a bad mood. Nothing is working and the words for what she wants to say will not come easily into her mind. Memory has forsaken her, or so it seems, though she knows she could pull out old class photos and name every person—the ones who mattered, the ones who fell into obscurity. Alive or dead, they populate the past, and she is angry at the present, her apparent failure to find an adjective, the right one, the one that would call up a color

THE CIRCUS TRAIN

or sound and convert static scene into vibrant motion. So her voice follows her through the house, towing its high-pitched register as the deer leaps the fence, the stream sluices between rocks, the ball arcs into the net, the hand reaches out to touch the cheek, and the heart lifts its—ah, that's it!—faded balloon of reciprocity.

What if we hadn't moved west, but stayed in the land where winter turned our streets into vast white fields? What if we—the he and the she—had never met? The story needs a beginning for it to end.

There was a he and an I and we spent the autumn living our rented life. Log house, steeple in the valley, smoke rising from somewhere in the east. Cows wandered down the road until their owner chugged his way up the hill to force them back to where they oh so slowly came from. The season turned and we turned with it. It was a way of being someone else. Words crept across the page as though we could cash them in. We vowed we would never go back to the humdrum, though how long would it have taken for this to become our everyday life?.

JUDITH KITCHEN

Leaves—striated, their veins almost ours—
rose in a vortex of yellow and red, then
settled, rose again to the sound of distant
geese. We could not reconcile that migratory
cry with a world of sidewalks and calendars,
its almost-sorrow suffusing the air until the
"most" was swallowed by the "all" and nothing could concole us.

One, two, three and the hand flies out, fist
of a hand, rock to crush the scissors that cut
the life into two. Rock that fills the stream.
Brooks no nonsense. Rock with which to
build, fist upon fist, the layered wall that
crosses the moor. The moor with its open
ending. What / if / we / what / if / we, like a
huffing locomotive, what if we stepped back
into our perfect childhoods where winter
took your breath away as you stood there,
cold at the center, as snow slipped from the
branches and landed without sound at your
feet? Where wind made itself known as a
feather of snow, lifting, then settling, mere
tether of sound and you stood there looking
at a future swept clean of desire.

This is the power of imagination: A man is
entering Ipanema—the Brazilian restaurant

THE CIRCUS TRAIN

on 46th—where she herself is heading. Their paths are bound to cross. Finally it is happening. This time she is sure. The walk. The turn of the head. The open face. Surely she must have crossed his mind now and then. How has he imagined her? Is she the person he would like her to be? It will all be so easy. Just step through the door. And then she doesn't want it any more. He's just as she had imagined, and she doesn't want him any more. It's over. All these years of waiting, gone, like that.

But not gone surely since they never were. She lived those years in another place, another time, lived in Scotland, Brazil, with her husband and sons. Lived intensely in yet another life as when they—the he and the she of the story—resurrect themselves in Kodachrome. Intent on being individual, divisible by lives led apart, moments when he touched her cheek, that one moment when she drove away blinding tears so who knew what could happen the viaduct solid above its concrete abutments the large trees bending in wind so surely there would be nothing left of her to cry out in the rain surely there would only be the wind and the wishing for what would not come not then at least while the

JUDITH KITCHEN

pronouns held themselves apart like magnets pushing against each other the force so
palpable in the palms those little childhood
magnets tiny red horseshoes with silver tips
the ones that come in Christmas stockings
more fun than the more expensive toys and
isn't that the way of it that you like something better than what you are supposed to
like isn't that human nature at work so long
before the night she drove away . . .

That's what she wants—hot-flash of idiom—
to bore so deep into the mind that punctuation is unnecessary. Nouns and verbs all lost
to the velocity of words freed from syntax.

THE CIRCUS TRAIN

III.

Forever you go towards silence further and further,
it at once calls and repels. If we stay there
long enough nature draws us into the mood
of the infinite and the unknown.
—Edna O'Brien, *Mother Ireland*

In the background throb of happy hour—
second heartbeat—the music is restless.
Where is the resonance of water and wind?
A single brown bird? Or simple clarinet? She
does not want this raucous bark with its hint
of coyote. Its glint of fear.

One, two, three and the hand flies out, two
fingers split into a V. Scissors to cut through
the paper on which the story is unfolding.
Unafraid of the power of the word. One,
two, three and there you are—severed from
the person you would like to be. You are
left with who you are, guilty of what you've
said and done, said and done. You are all you
have, and yet you could not swear you'd recognize your signature. Your blue glass goblets, your Russian dolls, the books on your

shelves that tumble and mix inside you. The fingers split and you lift out of yourself, like geese that take to the air, gripping the air as though they could pull themselves *going, gone* into its body.

Forty years after the flood, we stood together watching water rising imperceptibly on my childhood until—whoosh—it crept over the dike, the street all aslosh. There it was on Youtube: the crumpled yellow arches of McDonald's, and Bonady's grocery spilled onto the streets as though it had been raining apples and bananas. There's Tillman's Drug Store—its green-and-white-striped awnings—ripped from their moorings and washed up downstream—downstreet—in the front yards of people who'd lost their belongings to weather. Forty years ago, we tugged sodden insulation from between the studs and rinsed rugs with hoses or wiped with soggy rags and still the damage was everywhere. What was the mood of that rain that fell and kept falling? Tioga, Cohocton, Chemung, Canisteo, Allegany, Susquehannah, as though centuries of Iroquois had risen in unison chanting their claims, possessed with deluge, destruction,

THE CIRCUS TRAIN

debridement: history washed back to one soundless canoe under the shade of this tree where we took shelter. The deep, dark rift of it.

Today we passed a tractor making its way through long grass, and in its wake, old-fashioned bales of straw like little rectangular building-blocks scattered across the landscape. Summer bound in twine. Stacks of heat. The circling hawk observed our short passage, a blink on the topographical map in his eye. This is his province: mouse, rabbit, vole, field the color of sun.

What if the film had wound itself through the camera? What if what I saw in my head had ended up as an image in my hand? Full-color, head-on. Who knows what I might have done with all those waving flags at dusk, samba winding its way up the hillsides, favelas with their drumbeat. Forget the dark undersides, forget the men who sleep in doorways, the children who beg for money, the children who will not go away, who will never go away. Though they have long ago grown up and gone away, riding the thermals of need.

JUDITH KITCHEN

Is this how a life adds up? The what-never-happened along with what did? The thoughts that race through the head? The colors and smells, peripheral, yet somehow seeping into the scene, caught as something—a presence—beyond the frame. Blast of light: the photo you might have taken on the film that didn't thread. The silent thread of a life, following you forward in time, as you fumble your way toward whatever comes next. Pure color, pure DNA of the spectrum—without tint or shade—anchored to absence.

There were two, as in any good story where people revolve around each other. Two cups and two plates. Two differing dreams. Two ways of measuring the future. Every sentence reminded her of the lack of the verb to be. Every sentence she spoke cut off at the point of projection.

Absence grew between them on its slender stalk. Husk of what they hadn't done. There was a he and a she. That was the constant. Together, a "we." But even within the shared life there was always the one that was lived in isolation. The one with paths that forked, then forked again, harking back and then back into a past that could not catch up. Within that shared life, an I that sees what it sees in its own stubborn way, that speaks in a voice you could only call yours, sequestered in its splendid sounds, the ear with its intricate casings.

You hunger for foghorn and woodthrush and the steady drip drip of snowmelt. Scuffle of sneakers through gravel. The unmistakable squeak of a rusty chain. You talk to yourself so you won't hear silence calling. Talk to your singular self, trapped in the clock's piercing shadow.

Surely she can't write it all before the renegade cells catch up with her. But what to do with merciless memory—sliver of time just under the surface of the skin? How her mother made her cut her own switch from the forsythia bush. The very word—*forsythia*—whiplash of sound. Or the time she forced her sons to go to a circus. Or the way the Allegany mountains go on and on, a rumpled quilt of blue hills receding. How it feels to peel a hard-boiled egg.

JUDITH KITCHEN

Hic, haec, hoc oiled floors, blackboard, chalk
huius, huius, huius we could have been *hī, hae,
haec* from any time *hōrum, hārum, hōrum* who
came and saw *divisa est* and conquered *in
partes tres* leaving almost invisible *hunc, hanc,
hoc* a road across the moor *hīs, hīs, hīs* trace
now obsolete *hīs, hīs, hīs* as men who wrote
their names on wax, on stone, sibilant hiss
of history.

There they are, driving through one of the
lives they didn't live. The trees are past
peak—darkly orange and brown, and on
the lawn the bright reds and yellows have
curled at the edges. Singed. Underfoot, they
make the sound of heavy wind, or the thick
rasp of a handsaw. The air is crisp and cold.
Overhead, the sky stretches blue, and con-
trails head straight upward, as though they
had zipped its halves together. They—the
he and the she—are driving past houses
they might have owned, and each FOR
SALE sign causes a twinge of nostalgia.
"Remember?" But what they remember is
the desire to walk through the door of each
house with a lit window, a bookshelf, maybe
a log on the fire. They don't remember shov-
eling snow because they left before it masked
the landscape. They don't remember the

fog, or the deliberate clouds that obliterated shadow. They do remember the river that parallels the road, its uneven stepping stones and the way the water rippled and surged, surrounding each stone with the noise of its passing. They remember who they were then—younger, more ready for the future. And here they are in that future, though it is now their present, and she cannot keep her balance on the stones, cannot make her hesitant way to the other side. Here they are, driving down Legate Road, away from the house they did not buy, though they picture the back room full of windows where they watched leaves dripping like rain in the forest, which now they call woods, having seen how deep and dark a real forest can be. They drive west, into the yellow hills that have long ago given them up.

Who will there be to say whether I became the person I wanted to be? Memory being what it is, there's no guarantee. So I write it here: I failed myself often, failed others as well. Failure, too, will fade. But words did not forsake me as they made their precarious way from the writer's mind to mine. If words were conditional, it was only in their transitory flight.

JUDITH KITCHEN

To have seen Pelé. To have lived in the era of
Messi and Ronaldo, to say nothing of Iniesta,
Di Maria, Adriano, Modric, Neymar. To have
watched the ball floating high in the bright
stadium air. To have tasted that intensity.
That pleasure. That unending forethought.

This house that holds us both. The he and
the she. This white house underneath the
Douglas fir. Late afternoon light that moves
with the breeze, currying favor. We are in it,
and of it. In our separate rooms, we whittle
at words while the life we are living slips
under the tree, spreads itself on the lawn.
The life we are living, caught in our words.
Our guilty lack of action. Our shamefaced
inwardnesses, those places where we never
meet. Or only meet. It's hard to know which
we would like it to be.

So what is her mood, now that she lives
with the word for her death? It will never go
away. And what is a mood, she wonders, and
how does that differ from tone? When will
she give up that narrator's stance? Simply
be. It sounds so simple. The mind at rest.
The sounds merely pitch. A steady periodic
sound to hold her here, an individual I on

this earth soon to lose the distinctions of pronoun. Left merely with a tone.

Atone.

At one.

Dedicated to Allan, Fleda, fellow travelers.

Thanks to Stephen Corey and Mary François Rockcastle
for believing in this form. Thanks also to Stephen
for making me learn the value of subtraction.

"The Circus Train" was first published in the Summer
2013 issue of The *Georgia Review.*
"Coda" appeared in the Fall 2013 issue of *Water~Stone
Review.*
A short excerpt from "The Circus Train" was awarded
first place in the *Open to Interpretation: Fading Light*
contest, Taylor & O'Neill, 2013.

Lines quoted from: "Ask Me" by William Stafford; "The
Man on the Dump" by Wallace Stevens; "A Dust of
Snow" and "West-running Brook" by Robert Frost; "The
Dead" by James Joyce.

Thanks also to the good company of my first readers—
Dinah Lenney, Sandra Swinburne, Cheryl Merrill, Sheila
Bender, Kate deGutes.

Judith Kitchen is the author of six books and has served as an editor for four anthologies. Her awards include a fellowship from the National Endowment of the Arts, two Pushcart Prizes, the S. Mariella Gable Award, and the Lillian Fairchild Award. For twenty-five years, she has acted as a regular reviewer of poetry for the *Georgia Review* and is currently working on a collection of selected reviews. A former director of the Rainier Writing Workshop, she now lives and writes in Port Townsend, WA—in the same time zone (but not the same zip code) as her three grandsons, Benjamin, Simon, and Ian, who can be found in the pages of this book.

OVENBIRD

Judith Kitchen's Ovenbird Books promotes innovative, imaginative, experimental works of creative nonfiction.

Ovenbird Books
The Circus Train by Judith Kitchen

Judith Kitchen Select:
The Last Good Obsession by Sandra Swinburne
Dear Boy: An Epistolary Memoir by Heather Weber
The Slow Farm by Tarn Wilson

www: ovenbirdbooks.org

7886086R00098

Made in the USA
San Bernardino, CA
20 January 2014